## At Issue

# | Gender Politics

# Other Books in the At Issue Series:

# At Issue

# | Gender Politics

Susan Henneberg, Book Editor

GREENHAVEN
PUBLISHING

Published in 2017 by Greenhaven Publishing, LLC
353 3rd Avenue, Suite 255, New York, NY 10010

Copyright © 2017 by Greenhaven Publishing, LLC

First Edition

Articles in Greenhaven Publishing anthologies are often edited for length to meet page
requirements. In addition, original titles of these works are changed to clearly present
the main thesis and to explicitly indicate the author's opinion. Every effort is made to
ensure that Greenhaven Publishing accurately reflects the original intent of the authors.
Every effort has been made to trace the owners of the copyrighted material.

Cover image: [TK]

**Library of Congress Cataloging-in-Publication Data**

t/k

Manufactured in _____

Website: http://greenhavenpublishing.com

# Contents

# Introduction

Among the various holidays and days of commemoration in the United States are two that pass by each year without much notice. Both days pay tribute to the efforts of women to achieve civil rights equal to those of men. The first day is August 26, designated by Congress in 1971 as Women's Equality Day. It reminds Americans of that day in August 1920 on which women in the US were first given the right to vote. A Joint Resolution of Congress also recognizes August 26, 1970, "on which a nationwide demonstration for women's rights took place." On the fiftieth anniversary of the passage of the Nineteenth Amendment, 50,000 self-described feminists sponsored a march down New York City's Fifth Avenue. Called the Women's Strike for Equality March, the event was sponsored by the National Organization for Women (NOW) and organized by NOW leader Betty Friedan.

## Women's Strike for Equality

The 1970 Women's Strike for Equality movement was momentous in many respects. Historians now refer to the time period between the late 1960s and 1990s as the "second wave" of feminism. The concept of women's rights was controversial in a country that was led by men. While the activists' demands extended over a range of rights, they identified three main goals for the march and the strike. They wanted free abortion on demand, equal opportunity in employment, and the establishment of round-the-clock child care centers. The August 26 march kicked off multiple strategies for the attainment of these goals, such as lobbying, legislation, and more public protests.

The goals of the Strike for Equality were not met, though progress continued throughout the 1970s and '80s. Title IX of the Education Amendments of 1972 prohibited discrimination based on sex in education, allowing millions of girls to participate in sports at their schools. Title IX has been invoked to protect students from sexual harassment and assault on college campuses. In 1973, the Supreme Court decision *Roe v. Wade* legalized abortion in all fifty states, though it did not make the procedure affordable for all women. The goal with the least progress has been in child care. Though Congress passed the Comprehensive Child Development Act in 1971 to set up local day care centers, President Richard Nixon vetoed it.

## Working for Equal Pay

In 2016, President Barack Obama designated April 12 as "Equal Pay Day," symbolically marking how far into a new year women would have to work in order to earn the same as men did the previous year. In 2015, women earned 79 cents for every dollar men earned. Though few economists argue that the gender gap exists, there is a lot of disagreement about the causes of the gap and what might work as potential solutions to the issues of unequal pay. Many economists attribute the pay gap to the price women pay for career flexibility. Because they are the primary caretakers for children and elderly parents, women often ask for jobs with more predictability, or drop in and out of the job market to meet the needs of their family. Other economists argue that while career flexibility might account for some of the pay gap, wage discrimination also causes women to be paid less for the same work as men.

## Work for Equality in US Still Ongoing

The annual Women's Equality Day and Equal Pay Day serve as reminders for many women that the battle for equal rights and equal pay is still ongoing in the US. Many women suffer harassment and sexism while working in occupations once confined to men only. In the tech industry in particular, it is difficult for women to achieve any kind of employment parity with men. Some people attribute the lack of women in technical fields to women's lack of interest and ability in math or science in the higher levels of education. Others contend that often girls are discouraged from succeeding in science, math, or technology and harassed by men if they do try to make inroads into male dominated fields. Overall, however, recent research is showing that more women than men are entering higher education and earning college degrees at a higher rate than men. Many women are optimistic that the gains in education will open more opportunities to break the "glass ceiling" that appears to limit women's pathway's to top leadership positions.

## Gender Issues Worldwide

The battles for gender equality in the US are mainly played out in classrooms, offices, and legislatures. Worldwide, the issues have much higher stakes and often include violence. In most developed First World countries, such as Canada, Australia, Japan, and most of Europe, gender equality mirrors that in the US. In countries less prosperous or developed, such as some in Africa, South America, and Asia, women struggle for basic rights such as access to education, freedom from discrimination, and safety from gender-based violence (GBV). Regional conflicts among different factions within a country tend to impact women disproportionally. Cultural traditions often condemn women to lifetimes of poverty and servitude.

## Education for Girls

Some parts of the world, such as rural areas in sub-Saharan Africa and Southern Asia, have low rates of girls attending school. For instance, statistics from the United Nations Educational, Scientific, and Cultural Organization (UNESCO) showed that in 2009 only 23 percent of girls in Somalia attended school, compared to 43 percent of boys. Worldwide, women account for two-thirds of the world's illiterate adults. Gains in girls' educational levels have large payoffs for poor families. According to the World Bank, "increasing girls' schooling boosts women's wages and leads to faster economic growth than educating only boys. Moreover, when women earn more money, they are more likely to invest it in their children and households, enhancing family wealth and well-being."

Educated women report lower levels of HIV infection, domestic violence, and traditional practices such as female genital mutilation.

## Gender-Based Violence

The World Bank and the World Health Organization (WHO) have recently begun projects aimed at addressing the problem of gender-based violence. These organizations estimate that 35 percent of the world's women have experienced some form of GBV, rooted in unequal power relationships between men and women. This violence includes workplace harassment, domestic violence, rape, female genital mutilation, forced abortion, sex trafficking, and honor killings. Physical injuries, psychological trauma, loss of employment, and the exposure of children to violence are some of the long-term impacts of GBV. International agencies such as the World Bank and WHO support educational initiatives, family courts, access to health care and community centers, and media campaigns, which can prevent or reduce GBV.

## Missing Girls

A particular problem in some countries, especially those with a cultural bias that favors boy children over girls, is female infanticide. India and China are the most visible examples of patrilineal societies in which transmission of the family and property occurs with boys. Daughters are married off to another family, while the sons and their wives are expected to care for parents in their old age. Before modern medical technology was developed that can determine the gender of a fetus early in pregnancy, female babies were killed or abandoned. Since the 1990s, ultrasound, DNA tests, and amniocentesis have been used to determine the sex of a fetus. Women can then decide to abort the fetus if it is a girl. Sex-selective abortions are illegal in many countries.

The issue of "missing girls" in parts of the world has alarmed many scientists and policy makers. According to the United Nations Population Fund, some areas in Asia have seen ratios as high as 130 boys per 100 girls. Preventing the birth of the next generation of women, experts predict, will have serious consequences. They fear that the competition for women will increase gender-based violence and human trafficking. The solution to gender-based sex selection, scientists, economists, and policy makers say, is the same solution for many gender-based problems. In her 1995 speech to the United Nations 4th World Conference on Women, then United States First Lady Hillary Rodham Clinton said that "women's rights are human rights." Clinton argued that when women are respected, educated, and allowed to achieve their full potential, the family and whole community benefits.

The articles in this volume reflect the wide range of issues surrounding the rights of women in the world today. From being attacked for their choice of professional clothing to being raped while taking a bus home from school, women face discrimination, violence, abuse, and life long trauma for nothing more than being a woman.

# 1

# US Women Trail the World in Political Equality

*Mia Bush*

*Mia Bush is a writer and editor at Voice of America, a US government-funded multimedia news source and the official external broadcasting institution of the United States.*

*Women in the US trail women in many other parts of the world in gender equality, ranking 28th out of 145 countries in an annual world survey of the equality of women. The US ranks 73rd in the percentage of women represented in the country's legislative body. It also ranks low in the percentage of women in business leadership roles. Women's access to health care is under threat with many states restricting access to family planning services. Despite earning more college degrees than men, women's pay remains stagnant.*

The beginnings of International Women's Day—a mass protest by thousands of women in New York City seeking better pay and working conditions, and the right to vote—have evolved into a day to take stock of the progress made toward gender equality as well as issues that still need to be addressed.

The United Nations views gender equality—the view that women and men have equal value and should be afforded equal treatment—as a human right.

"U.S. Women Make Strides Toward Equality, But Work Remains," Mia Bush, VOA, March 8, 2016. Reprinted with permission from Voice of America.

Yet despite a more than 100-year history for International Women's Day, discrimination against women and girls continues worldwide in the form of gender-based violence and discrimination.

## US Ranking

The United States has made huge strides since that first march in 1908: women won the right to vote, they make up about half of the workforce and they now earn a higher percentage of college degrees than men, among other things.

However, the U.S. rates 28th out of 145 countries in an annual world ranking of equality for women.

### The Gender Gap Worldwide*

| TOP RANKED | BOTTOM RANKED |
|---|---|
| 1. Iceland | 141. Iran, Islamic Republic |
| 2. Norway | 142. Chad |
| 3. Finland | 143. Syria |
| 4. Sweden | 144. Pakistan |
| 5. Ireland | 145. Yemen |
| 6. Rwanda | |
| 7. Philippines | |
| 8. Switzerland | |
| 9. Slovenia | |
| 10. New Zealand | |
| 28. United States | |

*based on economic, educational, health-based and political indicators.
Source: World Economic Forum, Global Gender Gap Index, 2015.

The report, which was first published in 2006, shows progress has been made in the past decade, yet inequalities remain. In fact, it notes the gender gap has closed only 4 percent in the past 10 years, and at that rate, it would take 118 years to reach parity.

Iceland ranks No. 1 in the report, a position it has held for the past seven years. The Scandinavian countries—Norway, Sweden and Finland—as well as Ireland round out the top five countries. At the lower end, Yemen ranks as the least equal country for women.

## Wages, Politics

The U.S. fell eight places in 2015, with the report citing a slight drop in wage equality for similar work and fewer women in leading government positions.

While former Secretary of State Hillary Clinton is a front-runner in the Democratic presidential nominating race this year, the U.S., with women holding just 26.1 percent of high government positions, ranks 29th in the world, according to a U.N. report, "Women in Politics: 2015."

It fares worse regarding congressional seats. The United States ranks 73rd—tying with Panama—with women holding just 19.3 percent of the seats in the U.S. Congress—84 in the House and 20 in the Senate.

### Women's Participation in Government by World Region

| REGION | PERCENT OF WOMEN IN GOVERNMENT |
|---|---|
| Europe | 25% |
| Oceana | 25% |
| Latin America and the Caribbean | 23% |
| Africa | 21% |
| North America | 21% |
| Asia | 18% |
| World | 20% |

*Source: Voice of America*

While the U.S. does well regarding three criteria of the gender gap report, "the political representation of women in this country is abysmal," Keshet Bachan, a girl's empowerment expert in Washington, D.C., told VOA.

"Just for comparison, Rwanda's female representation to their [parliament] is over 60 percent, and in the Netherlands it's almost 40 percent," Bachan said. "We've never had a female president, which further drops our score."

## Leadership in Business

The lack of gender equality extends to women in positions of leadership in U.S. businesses as well.

Just 20 years ago, there were no female CEOs of Fortune 500 companies, according to the Pew Research Center. In January 2015, Pew counted 26 women—5.2 percent—serving as CEOs of such companies.

However, women held nearly 17 percent of positions on company boards, according to 2013 data, up from nearly 10 percent in 1995.

In November 2014, women accounted for nearly half of the U.S. workforce—47 percent. The number of working women 16 and older steadily grew for three decades, increasing from 39 percent in 1965 to 60 percent in 1999, Pew found. But the number fell to 57 percent by November 2014.

### Gender Equality Rankings by U.S. State

| 5 TOP RANKED STATES | 5 BOTTOM RANKED STATES |
|---|---|
| 1. Hawaii | 46. Wyoming |
| 2. New York | 47. Texas |
| 3. Illinois | 48. South Carolina |
| 4. Maryland | 49. Idaho |
| 5. Vermont | 50. Utah |

Source: WalletHub.com

Education has been proven to be a strong equalizer between men and women, yet globally, nearly half a billion women cannot read and 62 million girls are denied an education, according to UNICEF.

However, education is an area where U.S. women have surpassed men. Since the 1990s, women have outnumbered men in college enrollment and completion rates, a Pew study found in 2013. Thirty-seven percent of women ages 25-29 had at least a bachelor's degree, compared with 30 percent of men the same age, according to Pew.

## College Degrees

Women are also more likely to continue in education after receiving a bachelor's degree: in 2012, women earned 60 percent of all master's degrees and 51 percent of all doctorates; in 2013, women earned 36 percent of master of business administration degrees, according to the Pew study.

However, despite the gains in education, a gender wage gap persists, and is even wider for minority women.

The median weekly earnings for full-time female workers were about 80.4 percent of men's earnings, according to fourth-quarter 2015 statistics by the U.S. Department of Labor.

In 2014, African-American women were paid 63 percent of what white men were paid, while Hispanic women were paid just 54 percent, according to a survey by theAmerican Association of University Women (AAUW), a group that advocates for equity and education for women and girls.

In 1979, U.S. women earned about 62 percent as much as men in the same position, the Department of Labor said.

AAUW's report, "The Simple Truth About the Gender Pay Gap," found the wage gap has narrowed in the past 30 years due largely to more women furthering their education and entering the workforce.

Nationwide, the pay gap was smallest in Washington, D.C., where women were paid 90 percent of what men were paid in

## Educating Girls

International Women's Day, while initially focused on women in the workplace, has evolved into a day to take stock of the progress made toward gender equality as well as issues that still need to be addressed.

Education has been proven to be a strong equalizer between men and women yet, globally, nearly half a billion women cannot read and 62 million girls are denied an education, according to UNICEF.

A report on girls' education noted that girls are kept from school for many reasons:

- Poverty
- Institutional and cultural barriers
- Pressure for early marriage
- Lack of safety in getting to school
- Lack of separate latrines for boys and girls
- Sexual harassment and gender-based violence in schools
- Domestic work overload

If girls receive an education, it leads to:

- A decrease in child marriages by 64 percent
- A decrease in maternal mortality by 70 percent
- More children surviving past the age of 5

2015, according to the American Community Survey, the ongoing statistical survey by the U.S. Census Bureau. The pay gap was largest in Louisiana, where women were paid 65 percent of what men were paid.

## Advances Made

In one of his first acts in office in 2009, President Barack Obama signed into law the Lilly Ledbetter Fair Pay Act, which prohibits sex-based wage discrimination. However, Congress has not passed the Paycheck Fairness Act, which would make it easier for women to challenge wage disparities.

"We've made strides in closing the pay gap, but we could do more," Bachan said, referring to a report earlier this month by researchers at Accenture that said becoming adept at digital technology would help women close the gender gap in the workplace. "So that's the good news," she said.

"The bad news is that women's health in the U.S. is under constant threat, especially their access to comprehensive sexual and reproductive health and family planning. The campaign against Planned Parenthood, and the way states like Texas are making it harder for women to access abortion clinics. These are direct threats to our ability to make informed choices freely about whether, when and how many children we want to have," Bachan said.

"In terms of international laws, this is a basic minimum standard, and yet in the U.S. it's so highly politicized it's constantly being undermined," she told VOA.

Twenty years ago, a global gathering organized by the United Nations yielded what many consider a defining moment in the ongoing fight for gender equality.

Hillary Clinton, who was then the first lady of the United States, took the stage in Beijing and, in a 19-minute address, laid out a simple but soaring equation. "Human rights are women's rights and women's rights are human rights, once and for all," she said as applause erupted.

Her speech—delivered September 5, 1995, at the U.N. Fourth World Conference on Women—distilled the concerns brought forward by 5,000 official delegates and at least as many other participants.

## Conference History

They challenged limits on women's and girls' education and health care, including reproductive health. Disparities in economic security, wages and inheritance rights. Violence against women, from domestic abuse to female circumcision to human trafficking.

# GENDER WAGE GAP

- The median weekly earnings for full-time female workers were about 80.4 percent of men's earnings, according to fourth-quarter 2015 statistics by the U.S. Department of Labor.

- African-American women were paid 63 percent of what white men earned in 2014, while Hispanic women were paid only 54 percent, the American Association of University Women, or AAUW reported.

- Earnings for both female and male full-time workers tend to increase with age, with a plateau after 45 and a drop after age 65. Women typically earn about 90 percent of what men are paid until they hit age 35. After that, median earnings for women are typically from 76 to 81 percent of what men are paid, according to the AAUW.

- As a rule, earnings climb as years of education increase for both men and women; however, while more education is a useful tool for increasing earnings, it is not effective against the gender pay gap. At every level of academic achievement, women's median earnings are less than men's.

- The gender pay gap persists across educational levels, even among college graduates, AAUW reported. As a result, women who earn college degrees are less able to pay off their student loans promptly, leaving them in debt longer than men.

- In 2014, the wage gap was smallest in Washington, D.C., where women were paid 90 percent of what men earned, and largest in Louisiana, where women earned 65 percent of what men were paid, according to the U.S. Census Bureau's American Community Survey.

Sources: **U.S. Department of Labor; American Association of University Women: "The Simple Truth About the Gender Pay Gap"; the American Community Survey; U.S. Census Bureau.**

This fourth women's conference made history, 20 years after the first, by securing the pledges of 189 world leaders to help females attain equality. Leaders committed to an action plan setting benchmarks and ensuring that women have "a full and equal share in economic, social, cultural and political decision-making" in public and private life.

"There was anticipation. There was excitement, too," recalled former U.S. Representative Connie Morella, who had led a small, bipartisan congressional delegation to the conference.

The Republican said she "felt the eyes of the world needed to look at what was happening to women.... I knew that my sisters in other parts of the world needed to have the protections I needed to have. In most instances, they needed them even more."

As Clinton noted in her 1995 remarks: "What we are learning around the world is that if women are healthy and educated, their families will flourish. If women are free from violence, their families will flourish. If women have a chance to work and earn as full and equal partners in society, their families will flourish. And when families flourish, communities and nations do as well.

"That is why every woman, every man, every child, every family, and every nation on this planet does have a stake in the discussion"—and in reaching those goals, she said.

Bachan is also optimistic that the goal of gender equality can be reached.

"The biggest win we could see is in encouraging more girls and young women to study STEM (science, technology, engineering and math) subjects and enter the tech industry. The stereotypes that discourage girls from studying engineering or mathematics are changing rapidly," she said, adding it is also up to tech companies to eliminate bias in their hiring practices.

"At the very end of that pipeline we still need companies to be more female friendly," Bachan said. "It's still very much a tech-bro space which alienates women. I'm optimistic, though, given the rise of girls and women in this industry, and looking to other sectors like law or female doctors, where we've seen huge increases in female representation in the past few decades means it can be done."

International Women's Day was first observed in 1909, but it wasn't observed by the United Nations until 1975. It's now celebrated in more than 25 countries around the world, from Afghanistan to Russia.

In 1981, the U.S. Congress established National Women's History Week to be commemorated the second week of March, expanding the observation to a women's history month in 1987.

Events have taken place in the days leading up to Tuesday's official day of recognition, when events are scheduled throughout the U.S. and the world.

# 2

## The Gender Pay Gap Remains Consistent Over the Last Decade

### Council of Economic Advisers

*The Council of Economic Advisers is an agency with the Executive Office of the President that advises the president on economic policy.*

*Despite comprising half of the labor force, in 2014 the median woman earned only 78 percent of what the median man earned. Women are less likely to have employer-paid health insurance or retirement savings plans. Some, but not all, of the pay gap is because of women's choices of occupations and family responsibilities. Some experts hypothesize that some of the gender pay gap is due to differences in pay negotiations and promotions and the secrecy in which many organizations keep their salaries and pay scales. Although the pay gap narrowed between the 1970s and 1990s, it has remained the same since 2001.*

April 14 marks Equal Pay Day, the day that represents how far into 2015 the average American woman has to work, in addition to her work in 2014, in order to earn what the average man did in 2014. In recognition of Equal Pay Day, it's instructive to take a step back and examine what we know about the pay gap.

"Gender Pay Gap: Recent Trends and Explanations," Council of Economic Advisers Issue Brief, April 2015.

## The Pay Gap

Over the past century, American women have made tremendous strides in increasing their labor market experience and their skills. Today, women account for 47 percent of the labor force and they hold 49.3 percent of jobs (women are more likely to hold two or more jobs and they are less likely to be self-employed). Women's share of the labor force has been rising for more than 50 years and is continuing to increase. Today more households than ever have a woman as the primary or equal breadwinner in the household. On Equal Pay Day, however, we focus on a stubborn and troubling fact: Despite women's gains a large gender pay gap still exists. In 2013, the median woman working full-time all year earned 78 percent of what the median man working full-time all year earned. Phrased differently, she earned 78 cents for every dollar he did. Although this gap generally narrowed between the 1970s and 1990s, it has largely stopped narrowing and has remained between 76 and 78 cents since 2001.

## The Compensation Gap

The pay gap goes beyond wages and is even greater when we look at workers' full compensation packages. Compensation includes not just wages, but also employer-sponsored health and retirement benefits, training opportunities, flexible work arrangements, and paid family and sick leave.

Women are less likely to have an offer of health insurance from their employer. Overall, women are also less likely to have retirement savings plans, however this gender gap is concentrated among lower income women. Prime-age women with college degrees are about as likely as their male counterparts to be covered by their employer's pension plan, while less-educated women are less likely to have an employer-based retirement plan. Being offered a retirement plan is only the first step in retirement savings. The next step is accumulating retirement savings and even among those with a retirement account, women tend to have lower balances than men, which is partially driven by the pay gap.

Women are also slightly less likely than men to have access to paid leave and, perhaps as a result, are slightly more likely to take leave without pay. The gap in paid leave is particularly large among workers without a college education: among these workers, 52 percent of men, but only 44 percent of women, have access to paid leave.

These broader measures of compensation show that the pay gap is not just about differences in earnings or wages: on numerous dimension— in access to employer-provided health insurance or pensions and paid leave, women's compensation falls short of men's.

But why do women earn less than men? Some people point to women's choices, some people point to discrimination, and some people point to differences in men and women's experience and education. There is no single answer, which is why we need to make progress on a number of dimensions. Let's break it apart so we can better understand what is driving the pay gap.

## The Gap from Education and Experience

Both education and experience shape what economists call "human capital"—the skills and qualifications learned either through education or on the job that make workers productive employees. In the past, men had greater levels of both education and experience than women, but this has radically changed since the 1970s.

While men were more likely to graduate from college in the 1960s and 1970s, in recent decades women have responded with greater force than men to the rising demand for education. Since the 1990s, the majority of all undergraduate and graduate degrees have gone to women. If these trends continue, women will represent a growing majority of our skilled workforce in the years ahead. These gains in educational attainment are particularly important for women's future earnings and employment. The wage difference between workers with a college and high school education has grown since the 1980s, and today, college graduates earn more than twice what high school graduates earn. And by some estimates, in just five years, two-thirds of all job openings will require at least some college education.

On-the-job experience is also an important determinant of wages, and in the past, women typically left the labor force after marrying or having children. Today, even though women are still more likely than men to temporarily exit the labor force, compared to previous decades, they are more likely to work throughout their lifetimes. For example, economists Francine Blau and Lawrence Kahn found that one-third of the decline in the pay gap over the 1980s was due to women's relative gains in experience. Today, even the majority of mothers with an infant are in the labor force.

Much of the decline in the pay gap that occurred in recent decades has been because women have closed education and experience gaps. In fact, since women have increasingly become our most skilled workers, after accounting for education, even more of the pay gap is unexplained. In fact, once we hold differences in men's and women's education constant, the pay gap actually widens today; 20 years ago taking account of differences in education narrowed our estimates of the pay gap. The gender pay gap tends to rise with education, with the smallest differences between the earnings of men and women with less education and the biggest gaps among those with advanced degrees. The pay gap among women and men with professional degrees is currently about 67 cents.

## The Gap from Occupation and Industry

As women's labor market participation and education increased, so did their career opportunities. Women have made tremendous progress in entering occupations that were once heavily male-dominated, part of what Claudia Goldin has termed the "quiet revolution."

Although occupational segregation has fallen, women are still more likely to work in lower-paying occupations and industries. Women remain underrepresented in the three industries with the highest average wages: information services, mining and logging, and utilities, but represent more than half of employees in the three industries with the lowest average wages: leisure and hospitality, retail trade, and other services.

Even when women and men are working side-by-side performing similar tasks, however, the pay gap does not fully disappear. Blau and Kahn decomposed the pay gap and concluded that differences in occupation and industry explain about 49 percent of the wage gap, but 41 percent of the wage gap is not explained by differences in educational attainment, experience, demographic characteristics, job type, or union status, using the Panel Survey of Income Dynamics. Using a similar approach, but newer data from the Current Population Survey, the Council of Economic Advisers finds that industry and occupation can explain about 20 percent of the wage gap, but about two-thirds of the gap is not explained by potential experience, age, race, education, industry, or occupation.

The real question, though, is why men and women end up in different occupations in the first place. It's not clear whether we should account for differences in industry and occupation in wage gap decompositions. If these differences stem from preferences, it is reasonable to account for them. On the other hand, if men and women choose different jobs because of discrimination, industry and occupation should not be included. In many situations, the line between discrimination and preference is ambiguous.

Take the example of computer science, where the share of women is lower today than it was in 1985. This gap doesn't start when workers are making career choices; rather, it results from a series of events and decisions that begin at very young ages. A recent OECD report finds that even high school girls who score high on math and science tests report low levels of confidence and proficiency in math and science. And once in college, women pursue science and math degrees at lower rates than men: in the 2013 school year, women received 57 percent of all bachelor degrees, but only 35 percent in STEM fields. Even among women who begin a science-related career, more than half leave by mid-career, double the rate of men. Forty percent of those who leave cite a hostile or "macho" culture as the primary reason. Given why women leave these fields, at least some occupational differences appear to be driven by negative factors that prevent the full range of talented Americans from succeeding in the workplace.

## The Gap from Family Responsibilities

At the early stages of their careers, each generation of young women has fared better than the previous generation. For example, in 1980, 18-34 year-old employed women earned about 74 cents for every dollar a man earned in an hour, but by 2013, this figure had increased to 87 cents. Reflecting increases in full-time work, the gap in annual earnings has narrowed even more. Some people point to this as evidence the pay gap reflects women's different choices and priorities.

One reason the gender wage gap has narrowed faster among younger women is that between 1980 and 2013, the median age of first birth rose from 22.6 to 26.0. Among college educated women, increases in the age of first birth have been even greater. Among women with advanced degrees the median age of first birth rose to age 31 by 2012.

Because motherhood is associated with a wage penalty and lower wage gains later in a woman's career these delays in childbirth have helped narrow the pay gap. Research has shown that delaying child birth for one year can increase a woman's total career earnings and experience by 9 percent. Yet men continue to experience pay increases when they have children. While economists have long speculated that these different experiences reflect household decisions about specialization and women with children do work fewer hours and are more likely to take parental leave, more recent research has documented patterns of discrimination against women with children.

In fact, once they have children, women do earn less and are more likely to leave the labor force. However, not all women who do so are doing it by choice. Research shows that when women have access to paid maternity leave, a year later they work more and have commensurately higher earnings. A lack of access to leave or affordable quality childcare prevents some women who would like to work from doing so.

This evidence all indicates that a lack of paid leave is particularly detrimental to women's long-term salaries and careers. Women are more likely than men to take extended time away from their careers when they don't have access paid leave that allows them to take temporary time off for the birth of a child. Research examining both maternity leave programs in other countries and in California concludes that paid leave can help new mothers maintain a connection to the labor force, and increase the likelihood they return to their employer.

## The Gap over Workers' Careers

In general, the pay gap grows over workers careers. Young people tend to start their careers with more similar levels of earnings, but over time, a gender gap emerges and grows.

This pattern exists across the spectrum of education and skills. For example, economists Marianne Bertrand, Claudia Goldin, and Lawrence Katz examined the salaries of MBA graduates from a top business school and found that although men and women had fairly similar earnings at graduation, after a decade, men earned approximately 60 percent more than women.

In their research they found that much of the growth in the earnings gap in the first decade was due to women being more likely to take time away from work—associated with child birth—and working fewer hours—also typically related to family and caregiving responsibilities.

In another example, Goldin found that law school graduates had similar earnings upon graduation. Although a small and insignificant pay gap opened after 5 years, it was similar among people with the same level of experience and working the same hours. After 15 years, however, male lawyers earned 55 percent more than female lawyers, and even after accounting for time out of work and job tenure, a 13 percent gap remained.

Therefore, even though gaps in work experience can account for some of the pay gap as women progress in their careers, a gap still remains between men and women with similar levels of experience, tenure, and credentials.

## The Gap Due to Differences in Negotiations and Promotions

As the pay gap grows over time, even for workers who don't have children, some have hypothesized that a growing gap is due to differences in negotiating salaries and receiving promotions.

In general, women, even highly-educated women, are less likely to negotiate their first job offer than men. But even when women do negotiate, if the norms of negotiation and salary expectations are not transparent, they are likely to receive less than men. While gaps in negotiated salaries are small in "low-ambiguity situations," in "high-ambiguity situations," women received about $10,000 less than similarly-qualified men.

Even though negotiation can lead to greater career prospects and higher wages, it can also be detrimental, particularly for women. Hannah Riley Bowles, Linda Babcock, and Lei Lai found that women were more often penalized for initiating negotiations, largely because female negotiators, while perceived as technically competent, were also viewed as socially incompetent.

While pay transparency can help reduce the ambiguity of negotiating situations, it cannot by itself eliminate the social penalties women face for initiating negotiations. Underlying all of the possible explanations for the gender pay gap is the potential for discrimination. This discrimination doesn't need to be overt: some work has suggested that implicit biases are more common. If implicit, or subconscious, biases are at play, a pay gap stemming from discrimination will be more difficult to overcome.

## The Role of Discrimination

It is difficult to isolate how much of the pay gap is due to discrimination. As this issue brief has discussed throughout, discrimination and implicit bias can impact the pay gap through many channels. It can influence what women choose to study in school, the industry or occupation that they choose to work in, the likelihood of a promotion or a raise, and even the chances that they stay working in their chosen profession.

Yet even when we ignore these forms of discrimination and hold education, experience, employment gaps due to children, occupation, industry, and job title constant, there is a pay gap. This "unexplained" pay gap leaves little beyond discrimination to explain it. Some research has found that this unexplained portion is a sizeable share of the total gap—41 percent.

While it is difficult to get a measure of discrimination from data sets, more experimental research is starting to show evidence of discrimination in hiring, pay, and advancement. Resume studies have shown that, among identical resumes where only the name differs, gender affects whether the candidate is hired, the starting salary offered, and the employer's overall assessment of the candidate's quality. These findings echo the conclusions of earlier audit studies. And even when women succeed in traditionally-male roles, studies find that women are perceived as less competent and likable than men.

More practically, the need for enforcement against gender discrimination in hiring, pay, and advancement is clear by the number of discrimination cases still being pursued and won.

## The Gap and Policy Implications

The President's proposals to ensure that all workers receive fair pay for a day's work do not hinge on the existence, or the magnitude, of a gender pay gap. These are common-sense policies that ensure all workers are treated fairly in the workplace and are able to select jobs that best match their skills, not their family obligations.

Since the beginning of the Administration, the President has prioritized eliminating workforce discrimination and enforcing anti-discrimination policy. The first piece of legislation he signed into law, the Lilly Ledbetter Act, empowers workers to recover wages lost due to discrimination by extending the time period in which an employee can file a claim. Many workers, however, are unaware whether they face wage discrimination. For example, a 2010 survey found that 19 percent of employees reported their employer formally prohibits discussing salaries and another 31 percent are discouraged from discussing pay.

A pay gap stemming from discrimination is particularly likely to exist under conditions of pay secrecy, where workers do not know whether they are being discriminated against. In order to improve pay transparency and ensure fair pay, the President continues to call on Congress to pass the Paycheck Fairness Act, which would enable millions of workers to discuss compensation without fear of retaliation. Last year, the President signed an Executive Order prohibiting federal contractors from retaliating against employees who choose to discuss their compensation.

Government agencies are also increasing collaboration and making interagency collaboration a regular component of their agencies' enforcement work. Agencies are also addressing the implications of pay secrecy norms and policies by focusing on how better data on pay can improve enforcement. The President signed a Presidential Memorandum last year instructing the Secretary of Labor to establish new regulations requiring federal contractors to submit to the Department of Labor summary data on compensation paid to their employees, including data by sex and race. The Department of Labor will use the data to encourage compliance with equal pay laws and to target enforcement more effectively by focusing efforts where there are discrepancies and reducing burdens on other employers.

Other policies that can help ensure fair pay include modernizing outdated overtime regulations and raising the minimum wage. When employers are requiring people to work long, unpredictable hours this can be particularly challenging for those who need to plan for childcare and other family responsibilities. Fair compensation for hours worked, access to workplace flexibility to shift either time or place of work, and advanced notice of work schedules can go a long way to making it easier for workers to balance their work and family responsibilities. Raising the minimum wage and the tipped minimum is particularly important for women since women are disproportionately represented in lower-wage sectors. Although women are 47 percent of the labor force, they represent about 56 percent of workers who would benefit from increasing the minimum wage to $10.10 and indexing it to inflation.

Family-friendly workplace policies can also better enable workers to choose jobs in which they will be most productive. Increasingly, mothers and fathers are sharing caregiving and family obligations, but many workplaces have been slower to adapt, and as a result, both men and women are voting with their feet. For example, work by Claudia Goldin shows that women are particularly likely to select careers that offer flexibility, like pharmacy or obstetrics. The demand for family-friendly workplace policies, however, is not limited to women. For example, nearly half of all working parents have reported rejecting a job because they felt the position would interfere with their family responsibilities.

Individual businesses and the economy as a whole benefit when workers are in jobs that are well-suited to their skills and qualifications. From a business's perspective, these policies can also increase worker productivity and worker retention. For example, in a study of over 700 firms, work-life balance policies were associated with higher productivity, and a survey of California employers found that 90 percent reported that paid leave did not harm productivity, profitability, turnover, or morale.

Moving forward on policies that ensure fair pay for all Americans and help workers find jobs that best suit their talents are key aspects of the President's middle class economics agenda. While these policies can help narrow the pay gap, they also allow businesses to attract and retain the strongest talent, which benefits the economy as a whole.

# 3

# The Gender Pay Gap Is Not Due to Discrimination

*Howard J. Wall and Alyson Reed*

*Howard J. Wall is an economist who formerly was vice president and regional economics adviser at the Federal Reserve Bank of St. Louis. Alyson Reed was formerly director of the Committee on Pay Equity.*

*While many economists agree that very little of the wage gap between working men and women is due to outright discrimination, some economists contend that discrimination might work in other ways. Women may be discouraged from entering male-dominated fields where they might earn higher pay. Women also feel societal pressure to take time off due to child-raising and family care, which impacts their earnings. Women may choose careers that trade flexibility in work hours for higher paying ones with more demanding schedules. Women of color earn lower wages due to both racial and gender discrimination.*

The response to economist Howard Wall's October 2000 article on the gender wage gap prompted some spirited feedback from readers. Among those we heard from was Alyson Reed, director of the National Committee on Pay Equity, who asked if we would consider publishing an alternative view. The following is a summary of Wall's original remarks, Reed's response and Wall's rebuttal.

"How Much of the Gender Wage Gap Is Due to Discrimination?," Howard J. Wall and Alyson Reed, Federal Reserve Bank of St. Louis, Reprinted by permission.

## The Gender Wage Gap and Wage Discrimination: Illusion or Reality?

*Howard Wall:*

Despite laws to prevent wage discrimination in the workplace, the median weekly earnings for full-time female workers in 1999 was only 76.5 percent that of their male counterparts. A close analysis, however, reveals that much of this gap is due to non-discriminatory factors:

- Weekly vs. hourly wages. Women typically work fewer hours a week than men. When you compare hourly wages, almost one-third of the gap disappears.
- Education, experience, occupation, union status. A 1997 study shows that men's educational and experience levels are currently greater than women's and that men gravitate toward industries and occupations that are higher-paying than women, including union jobs. These factors reduce the remaining wage gap by 62 percent.

The remaining 6.2 cents of the gap, which is unexplained, is the maximum that can be attributed to wage discrimination. Some of this unexplained portion might be due to the difficulties involved in accounting for the effects of childbearing on women's wages. For example, women aged 27 to 33 who have never had children earn a median hourly wage that is 98 percent of men's.

If it is flawed as a measure of wage discrimination, what do we make of the gender wage gap? Perhaps it is best used to indicate the underlying expectations and social norms that drive our career and workforce decisions, which themselves may be affected by other types of gender discrimination.

## Whatever You Call It, It's Still Discrimination and It Still Affects Women's Wages

*Alyson Reed:*

As Howard Wall notes in his article, the relationship between wage discrimination and the gender wage gap is complicated. As the national nonprofit coalition that has worked on this issue exclusively for more than 20 years, the National Committee on Pay Equity has tracked the debate, collected the facts and talked with women across the country about their experiences with discrimination on the job. This long-term involvement in pay equity issues informs our understanding of the complexities surrounding the wage gap and its use as an indicator of workplace equality.

I agree with Wall that not all of the wage gap is attributable to outright wage discrimination. He notes that differences in experience, training and occupation all contribute to the wage gap. I agree. However, it is important to understand whether the differences in experience, training and occupation themselves reflect larger workplace and societal discrimination. Indeed, Wall's point that other types of discrimination may have played a part in creating human capital and other differences between men and women is right on target.

The issue of occupational differences between men and women, and how the occupational segregation of these groups contributes to wage disparities, has been a focus of pay equity research. These differences may not constitute wage discrimination per se, but the disparities do reflect sex discrimination that limits the economic opportunities of many women. The issue of occupational segregation is a significant component of the wage gap because studies have shown that the more women are represented in a particular occupation, the less money it is likely to be paid. In other words, in a sexist society, the work of women tends to be undervalued.

The issues of experience and training are also significant. If women have less workplace experience than men do, it is typically because they have taken time out for family care-giving. In today's economy, women are still expected to bear the brunt of this responsibility. Furthermore, given their lower earnings, women are usually the parent in dual-income families who takes time off to raise small children. In this sense, the wage gap can become a self-fulfilling prophecy. Given the fact that the creation of an educated and secure workforce is one of the most important investments we can make for a strong economy in the future, it would be short-sighted for our economic system to penalize women for building the human capital of our youth.

Career preparation and training are also affected by gender norms. Women are encouraged to pursue certain types of work and discouraged from pursuing others. These gender role expectations can be very subtle, such as when the mass media stereotypes what is considered appropriate behavior for women, or they can be profound, such as when women enter traditionally male-dominated fields and encounter hostile work environments. Recent legal settlements indicate that women at Home Depot were discouraged from floor sales positions and steered toward cashier jobs, while male technicians at CBS were more likely to be offered lucrative overtime assignments than women. This hostility and subtler forms of resistance discourage women from pursuing non-traditional work opportunities. Recently, nine Ivy League universities acknowledged that women face barriers in the fields of science and engineering and pledged to remove those barriers.

It is also important to critique the notion that occupational differences merely reflect women's "choices." While some women may prefer teaching over police work, or a clerical job over a construction site, many women end up in jobs without making well-planned "career" choices in high school or college. The notion that most women look for job flexibility and "slow job skill deterioration" does not really apply to the vast majority of women in low wage or minimum wage jobs.

Although Wall's article did not address the racial wage gap, for women of color the intersection of both gender and racial discrimination in the workplace can be profound. For example, Hispanic women earn just 52 cents on the dollar compared with white men. While a portion of the gender wage gap is frequently attributed to women's occupational and lifestyle choices, this argument does not account for the wider wage gap experienced by women of color.

In the final analysis, wage disparities are just another indicator of the larger economic disparities between those with greater economic opportunities and those with fewer. Unfortunately, gender continues to be a significant factor in determining those opportunities. Until we have eradicated all vestiges of sexism in our society, the wage gap will persist.

## But Discrimination Is Hardly the Whole Story

*Howard Wall:*

Alyson Reed and I seem to agree that wage discrimination explains little of the gender wage gap. Instead, most of the gap can be explained by differences between men and women in average levels of various human capital measures—training, experience, occupation, etc. We also seem to agree that differences in these human capital variables could be affected by other types of discrimination that women may face at various stages of their lives and careers. Unfortunately, because of childbearing and child-rearing, it is difficult to separate the effects of discrimination from the effects of rational choices that women make about their work lives. In her response, Reed highlights these difficulties.

Reed mentions the negative correlation between the share of women in an occupation and the occupation's average wage, and, if my reading is correct, she implies that the causality flows from the former to the latter. The difficulty with much social science research, however, is that it is almost always impossible to draw such a causal conclusion from a simple statistical correlation.

This is what makes the determinants of the gender wage gap so hard to pin down. For example, women, for whatever reason, tend to bear a greater share of child care duties. Because of this, they might be more willing than men to trade wages for time flexibility, or to select occupations in which skills and wages erode relatively slowly in the event of an extended absence from the labor force. This means that jobs with relatively low wages but lots of time flexibility are more attractive to women than to men, and that there will be some relatively low-paying occupations with disproportionate shares of women. While my article does not espouse "the notion that occupational differences merely reflect women's 'choices,' " it does say that discrimination is by no means the only explanation.

One might argue that the fact that mothers are expected to bear a greater share of child care duties is itself a form of societal gender discrimination. While this is probably true, it is also probably true that other factors are important. For example, single-parent families are disproportionately ones in which the mother is present and the father is absent, meaning that the mother has no option but to assume the main role in child care and to bear the resulting labor market consequences. Similarly, because many babies are breast-fed, there are simple biological reasons for the mother to be more heavily relied upon. Finally, because husbands tend to be older than their wives, they will also tend to have more labor market experience and, therefore, higher wages. So, even if a husband and wife are in the same occupation and the wife faces no wage discrimination, the wife would have the lower wage and, because of this, might end up bearing more of the child care duties.

My original article concluded that, even if gender discrimination were eliminated, a gender wage gap of some unknown size—but smaller than the current one—would persist because it is determined partly by things other than discrimination. Reed appears to disagree with this in her final point, but this depends on what she means by "sexism." Nevertheless, I find ample evidence to support my original conclusion.

# 4

# A Universal Basic Income Would Provide Opportunities for Parents

*Anna Oman*

*Anna Oman is a public relations professional who specializes in political and legislative issues, the labor movement, health care, and parenting.*

*Some European countries are considering giving all citizens a basic income and health care that would provide a threshold amount enough on which to survive. Similar to US Social Security for seniors, this income would allow parents to stay home to raise children, which is currently uncompensated labor mostly done by women. This income would allow workers the flexibility to take entrepreneurial risks and pursue passion and creativity. It would also reduce the poverty rate and the stress suffered by working families.*

As the mother of two with a demanding career, I often feel stretched to my absolute limit. I see the same existential exhaustion in the faces of my fellow working moms: tired, frayed at the edges, not feeling satisfied with either our work performance or parenting. We shuffle from our cubes to the bathroom like zombies, pump breast milk under fluorescent office lights, wonder how the hell the laundry will get done, lament the fact that both baths for the kids and that project are overdue.

"What I Want for All Moms on Mother's Day: A Universal Basic Income," Anna Oman. https://medium.com/basic-income/want-i-want-for-all-mom-on-mothers-day-a-universal-basic-income-b3d1a67a030f#.jila5thc2. Licensed under CC BY-SA 4.0.

You see it in the headlines too. Increasingly full-time employees who are exempt from overtime pay are expected to put in well over 40 hours a week, gladly giving nearly every bit of our energy and productivity to our employer in exchange for a decent salary and benefits.

Where then does nurturing and raising our children fit in when both parents are on this merry-go-round of constant deadlines, ever-increasing demands? I know I struggle with it. I also understand that my struggles are nothing compared to those of moms that are raising kids on their own, or of moms raising families with pay at or near our paltry minimum wage.

Increasingly, I think of all the work that goes into caring for and raising children that goes completely uncompensated. I had been extremely privileged with both of my children to have the majority of my maternity leave compensated (by hoard and piece together vacation, personal, and sick leave). Only 12 percent of U.S. private sector workers have any paid family leave, thus most mothers must return to work shortly after giving birth.

### Countries with the Most Generous Maternity Leaves

| COUNTRY | PAID MATERNITY LEAVE |
| --- | --- |
| Bulgaria | 58 weeks |
| UK | 39 weeks |
| Slovak Republic | 34 weeks |
| Croatia | 30 weeks |
| Czech Republic | 28 weeks |
| Poland | 26 weeks |
| Ireland | 26 weeks |

*Source: OPEC*

Sadly, for most American moms, (even high earners) once her child is a few months old, the labor of that child's care (often 8–10 hours a day, 5 days a week of diaper changes, potty training, comforting, socializing, teaching, loving, and role-modeling) is outsourced to another woman who barely earns enough to care for her own family.

It's a tragedy for working moms and for the women paid to raise their children. Don't get me wrong, I am a huge proponent of women in the workplace. Women must have equal standing, equal pay, and equal treatment. It's an economic necessity for most women, and all women deserve the independence and control over their own lives that comes with being able to work outside the home and compete on a level playing field with men. I was raised by a single mom, who struggled to raise three children on a woman's earnings, always robbing Peter to pay Paul, barely keeping afloat with student loan debt, the mortgage, and our living expenses.

I remember reading an article in a women's magazine, *Cosmo* I believe, some years back. It featured advice from a very successful older woman to younger women about how to get ahead in the world of business. The pieces of advice that stuck with me:

1. Reconsider having children. But if you absolutely must, for the love of God, only have one child; and

2. Adjust your standards of cleanliness to your husband's low standards.

I didn't realize it at the time, but this very practical advice taps into a solution to the problem of avoiding as much as possible the uncompensated labor of caring. One can maximize one's lifetime earnings, the argument goes, by avoiding as much as possible the uncompensated labor of, for instance, walking the floors at night soothing a baby who won't sleep or cleaning the bathroom before your relatives visit. Reject the duty of the constant maintenance that a family requires—from soccer practice drop-offs to kids' dentist visits to loading the dishwasher—and you can shine in the workplace, it promises.

The problem is that life doesn't typically work that way. Surely, not having children is a valid option. Many women and many couples are choosing to forgo parenthood in favor of a child-free life. Still most people want children, and our society still needs people willing to have children, for the continuation of our species, if not for our economic and national security.

Many mothers have found joy and purpose outside of the traditional labor market—and so too are a growing number of fathers. They don't want to sacrifice 50+ hours a week to stay on the career track, and the truth is for many families, with the cost of childcare through the roof, it makes no sense from an economic standpoint. Nor is it the rational choice from the standpoint of the sanity and joy of a family.

A number of friends—truly brilliant women who had very promising careers—decided that raising more than one child and working full-time at the same time as their spouses was just not worth it. They're piecing together work that matters to them, producing a community newsletter, starting an online coaching business, writing blogs. But they're forgoing huge amounts of income over their lifetimes. They're far from lazy. In fact, they work their asses off.

In our current precarious world of work, this is both a luxury and a danger. These "opt-out" moms are only able to do so because they have a spouse who can support their families, and they often must cut their standards of living dramatically to make this choice work. Few women can afford such a "luxury" and, if the need arises because a spouse's income is lost, whether and how these women will be able to reenter the workforce full-time remains to be seen.

## So what is the solution to this mothers' conundrum? Universal healthcare and universal basic income.

A movement is sweeping Europe (where universal health care has been a reality for generations) to create a guaranteed level of income—not a fortune but enough to survive on—for every citizen. Swiss voters will soon considering a universal basic income, and Finland will pilot the idea in 2017.

With automation, we are moving toward a world—like it or not—in which many traditional forms of work will no longer be done by humans. At the same time, fewer people want the lifestyle of absolute self-abdication that's expected of overtime-exempt employees. So why not give every citizen a threshold income that they can survive on and allow them to create, work and live according to their terms?

While it sounds revolutionary, the universal basic income isn't a new concept for Americans. Alaska has had the closest thing to it in the world today for years with the Alaska Permanent Fund, an oil investment dividend for every resident. Thanks in part to this small annual payment, Alaska enjoys one of the nation's lowest poverty rates.

Social Security is another example. This guarantee of an income floor for seniors is widely recognized as the most successful anti-poverty program our nation has ever undertaken. This basic income doesn't mean that seniors sit around doing nothing all day. My mom's life improved markedly since hitting the age of Social Security and Medicare retirement because she now has the time and security to pursue her joy. She lives very simply, tutors local students, volunteers at the library, takes classes at the seniors center, holds a seat on the board of the local housing authority, participates in a book club, and is writing a novel.

Imagine if everyone was guaranteed healthcare and an income floor. People would still pursue their calling in life. In fact, they could do so more freely with more creativity and daring without the fear of not making ends meet. It would unleash the enormous creative potential that lays dormant within the hearts and minds of so many office workers, toiling away as their best ideas and dreams wither away.

It would also reduce the stress on working families—especially low-income families and single-parent households. Middle-income mothers and fathers could take a real period of leave to raise their children—part-time work would become a legitimate option for more people. And working men and women without children could more easily take a mid-career break, or a sabbatical, once widely recognized as the perfect antidote to burnout among big thinkers and the creative class (i.e. university professors).

As the nature of work changes, so too must our conceptions of it, and of our understand of the relationship between work, family and society. Job sharing, more small entrepreneurial efforts, teleworking—all of these things could be bolstered by universal healthcare and a universal basic income. All of them benefit working people, especially low-income families and parents struggling to balance meaningful work and the needs of their families.

A universal basic income would also put a small dent in the deficit created by the mountain of uncompensated labor done mostly by women—mostly by moms.

This Mother's Day my wish for all mothers is a universal basic income.

# 5

## Sexism Prevents Gender Equality in the Music Industry

### Stacie Huckeba

*Stacie Huckeba is an internationally recognized photographer and video producer. Clients include the Rock and Roll Hall of Fame Foundation, the Americana Music Foundation, and Sony Music Group.*

*Women working in male-dominated occupations such as the music industry often encounter sexist attitudes. Men sometimes make assumptions about the ability of women to understand complicated sound technology and act condescendingly. They act in ways toward women that would never be tolerated by men. Women feel that they would suffer repercussions if they fought back or complained. These attitudes can change if women find the courage to push back against sexism in any industry in which they are found.*

I walked into the venue and found the sound guy. I introduced myself, handed him my audio transmitter and asked if he could give me an XLR mix out. "Why," he asks. "I am filming the show and need clean audio." "Yeah, but what is this going to?" he asks. "A wireless receiver," I reply. "Who is running it?" "I am," I tell him. He wants to know where and if he can see it. "It's on the other side of the room. It's just a basic receiver. It's on and programmed. All I need is an XLR mix out. It's all dialed in."

"A Professional's Perspective On Sexism In The Music Industry," Stacie Huckeba. Reprinted by permission.

"Don't get b*tchy." He smiled. It didn't feel like what you'd call a friendly smile. He continued, "This is a direct board feed, you won't get much bass so you'll need a room mic." He seemed surprised that I knew, let alone had one already set up. Then went further. "The line I'm giving you is mono not stereo, someone will have to help you with that and the vocals are going to be hot. Hot means loud..."

And with his increasing condescension, I feel my ears turn red and I tuned out. When he finished, I say, "Got it, can you run this or not?" He plugs in the transmitter, and I hear "B*tch" under his breath as I walk away.

That happens more times than I wish it did. Funny thing is, when my male assistant asks, the answer is either "Sure," "Nope," or "Will a stereo line work?" I've never seen them say anything else, let alone take 10 minutes to give him a dissertation on what a board feed is, sounds like or what else he's going to need. And I've never heard them tell him, *Don't get b*tchy.*

I've worked in the music industry for over 30 years. In that time, my boobs have gotten me in serious trouble. Not because I've used them for anything or shown them around. I keep these babies on lock down. But they exist and people know it and sometimes they make me feel like they think I can't do my job because of them.

I was at a dinner party a few weeks ago and a woman who has been an executive with a world-renowned recording studio for 20 years walked in. When someone asked, "How is work?" She said, "Oh, you know, just trying to manage with my tiny girl brain." I howled—not only because the comment was funny, and it was, but because I knew all too well what she meant.

We've all read stories about female artists in the business. I Googled "Sexism in the music industry" and it yielded 610,000 results. Almost all of them related to female artists. When I reached out about this piece I was inundated with stories from and about female artists. What I couldn't seem to find were stories from women industry professionals—label heads, publicists, managers, visual artists like myself.

And once I started calling them, I realized this was a whole new ballgame. Many gave me stories, but all of them asked to remain anonymous or to not tell it at all because it would out them. They all felt like they would be fired, blackballed, it would get worse or it would perpetuate the b*tchy, slutty, crazy appellations they are already fighting. I understood it, but it bothered me.

We've all had those blatant moments. In the three decades I've been in this game, I've been manhandled, grabbed, groped and violated in inconceivable ways. I've thrown out torn clothing and cleaned bloodstains while I refused tears I was too proud to let fall. I've been called a whore, a tease, a groupie, a sycophant and everything in between. That sh*t is not ok, but I'm guessing none of it is news for any woman who works in a male-dominated field.

To tell you the truth, as bad as that stuff is, it's when my abilities come into question that I get pissed off. Defending my body can happen when I go to Walgreens, but when you dismiss my intellect or capacity to perform as a professional simply because I have boobs, that's weird, and you and I now have a situation.

I sat down with the woman I was talking about earlier, along with three other very powerful women in the music industry to discuss this topic. It was fascinating. We all felt marginalized, ignored, disregarded and disrespected in instances, where if the shoe were on the foot of a man with our credentials, it would never have happened.

The most fascinating part was that we all did the same thing in our girl brains. We questioned if we were actually on the receiving end of misogyny or were just being sensitive. "Did I imagine that or was it real?" The fact that we all thought it told me all I need to know.

I asked how we could change it. That was the only question met with uncomfortable silence and "hey, girl" shoulder shruggin'. Our careers revolve around music, which has always been the driving force behind change. It's the courage of the songwriter that plays in our minds when we hear a song that moves us. Be it political, personal or satirical. Artists are the people we get up and go to work for every day. How do we honor and respect them and not be that brave ourselves?

I certainly don't have the answers. I'm not even sure all of it is intentional. Some dudes have just always worked with dudes and some people make snap judgements. Never good. But I have noticed that more ladies run the show these days. And more women are stepping into the roles that have traditionally been occupied by men. That's good.

I'm going to start here. I'm going to put sound guys the world over on notice. Hey, sound guys, people with boobs also have the capacity to understand basic sound. There. I said it. Now, Do you have an XLR out or what?

# 6

# Women's Voices Are Silenced in the Tech Industry

*Vivien Maidaborn*

*Vivien Maidaborn is a founding member of Loomio, a group that makes open source decision-making software that fosters group collaboration.*

*The open source tech industry can be a hostile world for women trying to break in to what has previously been a male-dominated field. Women report being the target of threats and abuse and having their voices silenced when attempting to contribute to the open source community. Some women point out that women are 50 percent of the consumers of open source technology. They contend that the tech industry would benefit from the feminist values of diversity, collaboration, social justice, and security.*

It is a shock to join a new industry, one forging open thinking, open models of exchange, and open source only to discover how closed it is to women.

This post began on a journey with my colleague Ben through Europe and the US in late 2013, talking with other people in the civic-tech and open source world. Our conversations were focused on citizenship, direct democracy, diversity and open technology. In about week three I wrote the following in my journal:

Journal Entry, Berlin Dec 2013

"What has been shocking is how few women have been part of this journey, how much men have dominated the space, across countries and cultures. My senses feel assaulted with this assertion of masculine presence in so many ways.

The men who hear me ask a question but address their responses to Ben; the woman-hating art on the office walls of men with whom we thought we shared a vision for the future.

The men who interrupt women's conversation to assert their knowledge and expertise closing down the sharing already in play; the taking of physical space in buses and trains. In Strasbourg, even the youth delegation in our session, as wonderful as they were, were all men. I wonder if hearing and listening to the issues of youth is just one more priority that is more important than addressing the inequality of women, and the silencing of women's voices?"

Since coming home to NZ I have been paying attention more to what is happening for women in open source communities and in the wider technology world.

Women are silenced in many different ways in life; in the open source and tech world this intensifies because of repeatability, and ease of broadcast. For feminists arriving into open source networks the marginalisation is intensified because of the shock at the actual experience compared to the expectation.

Gina Trapani suggests a conscious desire to exclude women within many OSS communities, a theory which is supported by comments on the recent gendered pronoun debate on Github. Both of these articles emphasise that fact that sexism in the open source community is consciously upheld and also strongly contested. It seems that the forces resisting change are still greater than the forces encouraging and facilitating it.

## Who is in the room

The numbers of women in the tech industry, and particularly women engineers and coders tell us this is not an equal opportunity world. Google.org says they invest in increasing the diversity amongst people training in computer science, particularly women and under-served minorities because right now in the U.S. only 15% of computer science graduates are women.

## How are we treated

If you want to know how deeply some people object to strong powerful women's voices, the stream of online misogyny is the most obvious, widely broadcast and visible example. The message though is no different from what women experience in many situations. I am reminded how men yell at lesbians in the street, and vilify women who publically oppose male violence. The new thing here is the medium and the ease that misogynist messages are amplified.

The pathetic sameness of the message over the 40 years I have been listening to it, the shallowness and complete lack of intelligence does not detract from its success in controlling what women feel able to do, which groups to join or frontiers to cross.

There are well known situations where women have been attacked online, with the intent of silencing them. Feminist Frequency author Anita Sarkeesian found herself the target of threats and abuse after suggesting that society take a look at the over-sexualised potrayal of women in video games. Australian journalist Asher Wolf founded Cryptoparty and then left it on the basis of continuing misogyny and hatred towards women within and outside the party.

Thankfully, amid the blasts of hate mail and trolling of feminists' Twitter accounts, a movement of resistance to the oppression is also growing. While projects like Everyday Sexism are bringing to light examples of sexism in the advertising, workplaces and the corporate world, there are growing numbers of women opening up the conversation about sexism in the open source world and the internet. Take a look at Geek Feminism and Tech LadyMafia who are creating an international network of women becoming guardians of the space.

The UK Guardian article on the "4th Wave of Feminism" highlights some of women who have spoken out:

A chorus rose against online misogyny. Criado-Perez highlighted the string of rape threats sent to her on Twitter, writer Lindy West published the comments she received, ("There is a group of rapists with over 9,000 penises coming for this fat [b****]," read one), and the academic and broadcaster Mary Beard, Lauren Mayberry from the band Chvrches, and Ruby Tandoh from The Great British Bake Off, all spoke out on this issue.

## What do we value?

Journal Entry, New York Dec. 2013

It is so easy living in my own lesbian friendly woman-loving context to forget how quickly you become invisible and how diminishing it feels to be not seen or heard when you are right there in the room; to see my voice falling like empty air on ears not listening, and to experience the privileging of men's voices even when in themselves they reject that privilege. Perhaps most shocking is that even when asked to stop, some of these passionate and values-aligned men cannot hear anything except their own voice, spewing their own brand of self importance in an endless gush of loud advice and domineering confidence.

The privileging of male voices in the room is a more subtle way of silencing women in the open source community. In my observation, this happens in three ways:

- Women are socialized to listen carefully to men—our safety depends on it and we do it very well. Men are listening to women much less carefully and often not at all.
- Men tend to be in the roles and occupations that have either structural authority or are seen as the more important roles.
- Finally, power attracts. So when people see who has the power in the group, attention flows that way.

We tend to value roles that are dominated by men, and in the open source community that is the engineers and coders. It is clear we need more women in these groups, but we also need to value the roles that sit alongside the coders. Many of us aspire to inclusion and collaboration across diversity, but how many of us actually do the core muscle work? A good litmus test for open source organisations and teams to understand who you privilege in your team, is to play with these gender bias games. Understanding whose voice gets listened to in your group is a great start.

## Entertaining difference?

One argument is that women and men enjoy different social and work contexts; that there are good reasons why we might choose different roles and jobs, and even good reasons to work separately. While there may be some seed of merit to this argument, many who hold this view ignore the contextual factors of the abuse, bullying and lower pay women experience compared to men.

## Building a New Narrative

The narratives we tell around open source itself, are part of the reason people are not considering the gender politics of the community.

The prevailing pattern in human rights movements is to give importance to the issue itself—peace, indigenous rights, nuclear freedom, mining etc. This becomes the narrow focus, and the connections between issues, oppressions and contextual factors are lost. As early as 1960 this was being written about in the context of the peace movement, and many of the issues raised in this Feminist Magazine Solidarity article remain totally relevant today.

It is noticeable in the web, that most articles about open source focus on the technical issues; the new code or tool, the pattern of use and the growth data. Wikipedia defines open source without any reference to the inclusive ideals within which it is grounded. And PC World is equally uninterested in anything except the growth and impact for business. This reflects the male interest and bias in the narrative around open source software.

Even more lacking is the narrative about the collaboration required to build good open source software, and how to do that well with greater input from diverse voices. We are missing so many of the discussions on how the interactions with online community informs technology. This issue is addressed in the work Nancy White et al did for their book Digital Habits. In this narrative, the technology serves community—it is clear that community is the purpose. Which raises the question of what is being served by marginalising women in a community interested in collaboration and collective intelligence?

## Finding Collective Intelligence

Sexism exists in many (probably most) work environments, so why is it so critical to stamp out in the open source community? It matters here like nowhere else because open source is about collective intelligence; it presents an alternative to individualistic models of the economy and cultural life. Collective intelligence is an oxymoron if in the process it excludes half of the population.

There are fantastic reasons to use and develop open source software. It addresses the fundamental issue of the right information and connectivity, involves collaboration and delivers better software. The goals of feminism and the open source movement have much in common, and the community could learn a lot by embracing feminist values.

**Access and Diversity**—Open source software, tools and resources are being built for a diverse world, where 50% of users will be women.

**Openness**—Women's rights are human rights and the internet is a vital space for women's organising and participation across the globe. This aligns so closely with the intent and purpose of the open source community. We can build on each other's strengths to achieve greater social justice.

**Security**—Privacy and security in the net is being constantly improved, but often fails to consider the security issues for women. We need to use our particular skills, knowledge and experience to create safe internet spaces for women.

## The Challenge

The challenge of today is to make room for the complexity of new power relationships in our diverse societies. We need to recognise and respect both our differences and our similarities, as we will inevitably merge, separate, combine and retreat in the work of solving the systemic, interconnected, wicked problems of our time.

Women are an integral part of this work. We are deeply and profoundly affected by exclusion and marginalisation today as much as ever. The interface between the personal and political has long been a narrative that women bring to systemic change.

The collective intelligence central to collaboration and inclusive decision-making needs all of us. I once defined myself as lesbian separatist so I could grow an identity separate from general society. These days I recognise that overcoming separatist thinking is a key part of the solution.

Journal Entry, San Fransisco Dec 2013

"Half way through our trip I am woken up to the danger of dropping women's priorities, women's voice and women's work from consciousness. In this young and technological world I am working in, I feel like there is a subtle fight going on all the time for us to respect the powerful and important differences in the perspectives that women bring. Every day I see the tweets from the UN Gender programme reminding me about the work of many many women in the world. The daily work often defined by water, food, children, health of communities and the fight for safety, education and safe reproductive technology. Through the Women's Refuge work in NZ, we can see that it is still a deep cultural reflex to control women through violence and intimidation. I am reminded about the fight for life women face in a world where fundamentalist religion and patriarchy are growing—those twin deadly power-over paradigms that assume men are more vital and important than women. Women's voice, presence, involvement is not some nice to have, something to fight for after we have resolved poverty, or changed the way democracy works. Women are integral to the success of the open source movement."

# 7

## Ethnic Minority Women Are Excluded in the Workplace

### Human Wrongs Watch

*Founded by Egyptian-born Spanish national Baher Kamal, Human Wrongs Watch is a website that collects stories about the abuses of people and environment.*

*Ethnic women are discriminated against in the workplace at higher rates than men or more Western-appearing women. Women with ethnic-sounding names or who dressed according to ethnic custom reported higher rates of rejection during the job application process. Indigenous women also reported higher rates of unemployment and discrimination. Ethnic women are victims of overlapping strands of exclusion tied to national and ethnic origin, race, religion, and gender. Overcoming this discrimination can lead a business to new customers, a better reputation, and higher profits.*

E thnic minority women face double discrimination in the workplace because of their race and their gender. Many fail at the application stage simply because of their names," says a new report by the International Labour Organization (ILO).

When university graduate Jorden Berkeley, 22, began applying for a job, she was surprised to have no responses. Born in the

United Kingdom of Caribbean parentage, she never dreamed that her name might be a problem.

But a careers adviser suggested that she begin using her more English-sounding middle name—Elizabeth—in her applications.

"I was surprised by what she said but I put my middle name on the CV as well. I started to get back responses, not necessarily job offers but it went from nothing to getting interviews. It was quite an eye-opener. I spoke to friends and family and it's a common occurrence. I've also read reports of Muslim women taking off their hijabs to get a job," Berkeley told ILO News.

## Black, Pakistani and Bangladeshi Heritage Women

Zunade Wilson, 22, also of Caribbean origin, had a similar experience, getting more callbacks when she used her middle name, Renatta. When she started working as a classroom assistant, she says she also faced discrimination.

"I wear my hair natural, in an afro. We were coming up to a school inspection and I was told that while the inspectors were there, I should do something with my hair, that I needed to make it neater. I said that this is how my hair grows and that I was not going to straighten it to please her."

A UK parliamentary report, Ethnic Minority Female Unemployment: Black, Pakistani and Bangladeshi Heritage Women said that in 2011, the overall unemployment rate for ethnic minority women in the UK was just over 14 per cent, more than double that of white women and higher than the unemployment rate for ethnic minority men.

Among Pakistani and Bangladeshi women it rose to 20.5 per cent. Many in this group reported being questioned about their intentions regarding marriage and children because of assumptions based on ethnicity, said the report.

## Latin America, Asia

In other parts of the world, particularly Latin America and parts of Asia, indigenous women are often discriminated against when they enter the labour market. Sometimes they are ridiculed and are subject to verbal and physical abuse for wearing their traditional dress in the workplace.

"Indigenous women all over the world experience discrimination, not only on the ground of sex, but also because of their indigenous identity, ethnicity, colour or religious beliefs. This multiple discrimination is particularly evident as women, particularly young indigenous women enter and try to advance through the labour market," says Jane Hodges, ILO Gender Equality Director.

## Persistent Multiple Discrimination

More than 170 countries have ratified the ILO's Convention 111 on non-discrimination in employment, which dates back to 1958. Yet the latest ILO report on Equality at Work found that discrimination continues to be "persistent and multifaceted," and has worsened with the global economic crisis.

"Discrimination has also become more varied, and discrimination on multiple grounds is becoming the rule rather than the exception," the report said.

According to a separate ILO study on multiple discrimination in many parts of the world, racial profiling targeting Muslim men and dress codes targeting Muslim women in the workplace have become more common amid the global political tensions following the September 11 attacks in the United States in 2001.

## Ethnic Diversity in Workplace

The difficulty, say researchers, is separating the overlapping strands of exclusion linked to national and ethnic origin, race, religion and gender.

Lisa Wong, ILO senior non-discrimination officer, says that the ILO has identified racial discrimination as a priority concern.

She is overseeing the production of a guide on promoting ethnic diversity in the workplace, which was pilot tested in South Africa at the end of January 2013.

"In spite of long-standing and well-established labour laws governing discrimination based on race in both industrialized and developing economies, discrimination on this ground, particularly where it intersects with sex, continues to be a challenge," Wong says.

The guide will provide simple policy recommendations such as conducting an ethnic diversity audit, drafting and implementing a diversity policy, and advice on how to work with employers and workers' organizations to raise awareness and improve managers' ability to effectively resolve complaints.

"When correctly implemented and managed, these steps can lead to not only a more diverse workforce, but also to improved accessibility to new and diverse customer markets, which can affect not only a company's reputation but ultimately profits," Wong added.

# 8

# Women in Power Are Constrained by Clothing Choices

## Jane Goodall

*Jane Goodall is an adjunct professor with the Writing and Society Research Centre at the University of Western Sydney and the author of both fiction and academic books.*

*Many women in powerful positions, such as prime ministers, US senators, or corporate CEOs, often feel obligated to imitate the masculine convention of dressing in business jackets. Some people contend that the jacket represents a larger issue. Women in jackets conform to male standards and stereotypes of female leadership, thereby not offending anyone or opening themselves to criticism. Some people encourage women to feel empowered to break the mold and dress in ways that more express their creativity and individuality. Rethinking the jacket may allow men and women to rethink the role of women in power.*

Germaine Greer had been responding to a questioner on the ABC's Q&A program (March 19, 2012), who asked what advice the panel would give to the Prime Minister Julia Gillard on her image problem.

Gillard's style was dry and somewhat terse, Greer said, but there were lots of good things about her. She was an administrator, who knew how to get things done. "It's unglamorous, it's not star material but it's what she's been doing… What I want her to do is get rid of those bloody jackets!"

The last comment was a flash of mischievous insight that seemed to take Greer herself by surprise, following the rather sober way she'd approached the question. Clearly enjoying the instantaneous response from the studio audience, she added: "They don't fit." If only she had stopped there, but by now the impulse to stir was irresistible. The jackets didn't fit because they were cut too narrow in the hips. "You've got a big arse, Julia. Get over it." That was the line that went viral, and Greer was widely condemned for a betrayal of feminist principles. At her next appearance on Q&A, she was called to account but was unrepentant, and provoked a kind of scandalised hilarity as she expanded freely on the matter of the Prime Minister's body shape and the need to rejoice in the fullness of female anatomy.

Somewhere in all this, a genuine insight was being lost: that at some level, the cut of the Prime Minister's jacket does matter, and that to get it wrong signals a lack of one of the many competencies required in the role. Greer's fix on the jacket question is in line with her fierce concern for technique and construction across a whole range of things, from car engines to Shakespeare sonnets. As a literary scholar, Greer also has a finely tuned instinct for metaphor, and at that particular stage in the political cycle, Julia Gillard risked looking as if she was not cut out for the role of prime minister; her preference for over-sculpted jackets bearing no comfortable relationship to her body shape served to underline the impression that there was a lack of fit.

It is quite possible that a change of style for a female political leader could help to reverse a slide in approval ratings, but Germaine Greer was making a more particular point before she veered off track. She was, quite explicitly, targeting the jackets, and the exhortation was not to get better ones but to get rid of them. This, when you think about it, was a bold and radical piece of advice. A political leader with no jackets?

As a garment conceived to give form to the human silhouette, the jacket expresses a relationship between form and formality; and as a staple item of business attire, it is a mandatory part of the western male dress code for formal occasions. Women have other options, but women in prominent political roles have generally resisted exploring them. There is a feminist issue here, though not the one that was running in the blog lines about the exchanges on Q&A. The earnest principle that professional women should not have to deal with a primary focus on their appearance has become over familiar, and Greer was deliberately flouting it, but in doing so she may have touched on a more interesting question: a question about the relationship between male and female dress codes and the ways in which power roles are culturally defined.

There are examples of female political leaders from non-western cultures who have adapted traditional female dress to create a personal image free of any suggestion that they are in roles defined by masculine conventions. Benazir Bhutto and Aung San Suu Kyi show how a woman in long skirts of beautiful fabrics, with a veil over her head or flowers in her hair, can look strong, elegant and distinctive. Yet western dress conventions for political leaders of both sexes are based on masculine traditions of business attire, in which the suit works to standardise the personal silhouette, creating smooth, subdued outlines for the lower body and with all the visual accent on the collar area, to draw attention upwards to the face. There is a literal aspect to focusing on the "head" in business. Attempts to feminise the look—through diversified approaches to the cut of the jacket, the introduction of bold colour in fabric choices, and the addition of pearls and crusty brooches—only make the anomaly more conspicuous.

## "Dress for Success"

What is called "power dressing" is essentially a phenomenon of the 1980s, belonging to the culture of social conservatism, economic rationalism and corporate ambition associated with that era. Following the publication of John T Molloy's book Dress for Success in 1975, the image of the career woman gained increasing currency, but it was Margaret Thatcher who really established the look. When she stood outside 10 Downing Street in May 1979, prepared to cross the threshold as the newly elected Prime Minister, Thatcher's appearance was contrived to go with an artificially softened voice and sentiments to match. Against the black stone of the building and the grey of the London street, the vibrant blue of her suit, complemented by a light print blouse, still carried vestiges of a prettiness belonging to a former era. The short jacket, contoured around the waist, and mid-calf skirt flaring out in sunray pleats recalled Dior's 1947 "new look," and the return of a womanly silhouette after the austerities of the war years.

As she grew firmer and more assertive in the new role, her suits evolved accordingly. Lapels were accentuated with contrast fabrics, shoulders widened, skirts straightened, blouses were tied off with a flourish in outsized bows at the neck. The blues intensified, becoming more royal, and alternating with black and white or red as chromatic anchors. Her hair was swept higher and wider around the temples so that her head quite literally seemed to expand.

These tendencies coincided with general trends in the fashion world of the 1980s, a decade in which the hippie ideals of the postwar baby boom were abandoned and Generation X focused on the competition for advancement on the corporate ladder. Thatcher set out to be the mould of form but not the glass of fashion; her image served to define the conservatism she expressed in her policies and every outfit she wore was 'on message'.

Over the ensuing decades, though, the message appears to have got lost somewhere, as leading women from both sides of politics continue to observe a dress code that is caught in a timewarp. Some obvious factors come to bear on the choices they make. Politicians who are at the mercy of constant opinion polling are understandably risk-averse in the business of creating and maintaining a public image, and women in positions of corporate leadership must command the confidence of peers and shareholders. The shifting aesthetics of the fashion world are dangerous ground for those who must project a sense of stalwartness and personal consistency, so a look that is only marginally influenced by style trends is the safest option.

For those who work an exhausting schedule involving international commitments, there is also an aspect of sheer convenience. Hillary Clinton's adoption of the pantsuit as a personal uniform is a way of opting out of the whole business of personal styling, in order to concentrate on matters of larger importance.

Angela Merkel, with a similar approach, has a range of long-line jackets in different colours, all cut to the same pattern and worn with black trousers. Such conscious stylists as Christine Lagarde and Condoleezza Rice are more various in their choices, but operate within the same set of conventions, assembling their outfits around versions of the sculpted jacket and fitted skirt or pants, accessorised with pearls.

## Power Dressing Paradox

So-called power dressing is a vexing paradox. It is associated with risk avoidance rather than adventure, conformity rather than trail blazing and innovation. It is a form of stylistic paralysis. In December 2012, Hillary Clinton addressed delegates at the NATO headquarters in Brussels wearing a jacket with edged lapels that might have cut on the same pattern as many of those in Thatcher's wardrobe. It's curious that women in powerful positions choose to present themselves in a style that is an anachronism even as they grapple with the most urgent issues of the moment in an endeavour to set directions for the future.

When it comes to offering advice on the image challenges of the Australian Prime Minister, a call for "the real Julia" has caused enough problems already. But perhaps this also points towards the heart of the matter. One of the hurdles for any woman who sets a precedent in a leadership role is the sneaking suspicion that she is not the real thing, but positions of power necessarily involve role play. There is no getting away from it, and there are weaker and stronger approaches to fashioning the role. The fact so many women in key positions are still trapped in the codes of power dressing is a reflection of the degree to which modern democracies shackle those in leadership to a set of negatives. In politics, those who live and die by opinion polling cannot afford to offend or confuse. They must never appear eccentric, or be open to accusations of inconsistency.

To break out of the negative cycle involves projecting courage and a sense of sustained inner conviction, and being able to capture the imagination of the public with vision and inspiration. This is where there is something to be gained in revisiting the dramatis personae of female theatres of power.

## "Get rid of the jackets!"

The trouble with Gillard's clothes, Germaine Greer said, is that they don't look as if they belong to her. How can those women who have followed Thatcher on the world stage expect to generate an effective presence if they persist in wearing clothes that belong to Margaret Thatcher, and that were designed to be on message for an intensely conservative politician of the 1980s? Presence is about being in the present, and a political leader should look as if their energies are drawn from the here and now.

Generational change is a factor that is due to come into play here. I got my first professional appointment as a lecturer in 1983, and celebrated by buying a pantsuit. At the time it was an exciting but acutely stressful transition in my life and looking back on it, I'm aware of how I was part of a wider social transition, as for the first time it became the norm for women in early adulthood to see their future in terms of career goals. We need to reflect on how recent this is, as a social and cultural transformation. The identity-shift for women is still in a phase of relative immaturity, but we need to look back as well as forward in order to find future directions.

Second-wave feminism took its impetus from an overblown critique of the status quo. Women were perceived to be essentially disempowered, and traditional forms of feminine control came under suspicion as being born of constraint, and having their basis in manipulative sexuality. As a consequence, the career woman of the 1980s who set out to be everything she could be was a figure cordoned off from deep and various traditions of female power. All those witches, queens, courtesans and divas were to be banished from our imaginative world. Banishing the jackets might help to prompt a more fundamental process of rethinking what women of power have been and may become.

# 9

## Educating Girls and Women Has Huge Payoffs

*Lori S. Ashford*

*Lori S. Ashford is a freelance consultant and has written about global population, health, and women's issues for twenty years. Formerly with the Population Reference Bureau, she authored the widely disseminated "Women of Our World" data sheets and the population bulletin "New Population Policies: Advancing Women's Health and Rights," among other publications.*

*Many developing countries are finding that educating girls results in families that are smaller, healthier, and better educated than families that don't educate their girls. Investing in girls' education leads to faster economic growth, lower levels of HIV infection, and a reduction in domestic violence and harmful practices toward women, such as female genital mutilation and bride burning. Girls still lag behind boys in countries where overall school enrollments are low. Countries can improve the education of girls by removing barriers such as school fees, early marriage and childbearing, and poor school quality.*

Few investments have as large a payoff as girls' education. Educated women are more likely to ensure health care for their families, educate their children and become income earners.

The right to education for all has been an international goal for decades, but since the 1990s, women's education and empowerment have come into sharp focus. Several landmark

"Women and Education," by By Lori S. Ashford , US Embassy, September, 2012.

conferences, including the 1994 International Conference on Population and Development, held in Cairo, and the 1995 Fourth World Conference on Women in Beijing, placed these issues at the center of development efforts.

The Millennium Development Goals—agreed to by world leaders at the U.N. Millennium Summit in 2000—call for universal primary education and for closing the gender gap in secondary and higher education. These high-level agreements spawned initiatives around the world to increase girls' school enrollments. Changes since 1990 have been remarkable, considering the barriers that had to be overcome in developing countries.

In many traditional societies, girls are prevented from attaining their full potential because of lower priority placed on educating daughters (who marry and leave the family) and the lower status of girls and women in general. Families may also have concerns about the school fees, girls being taught by male teachers and girls' safety away from home. Governments and communities have begun to break down these barriers, however, because of overwhelming evidence of the benefits of educating girls.

## Why educating girls matters

Few investments have as large a payoff as girls' education. Household surveys in developing countries have consistently shown that women with more education have smaller, healthier and better educated families. The linkages are clear: Educated women are more likely to take care of their health, desire fewer children and educate them well, which, in turn, makes it more likely their children will survive and thrive into adulthood.

Research by the World Bank and other organizations has shown that increasing girls' schooling boosts women's wages and leads to faster economic growth than educating only boys. Moreover, when women earn more money, they are more likely to invest it in their children and households, enhancing family wealth and well-being. Other benefits of women's education captured in studies include lower levels of HIV infection, domestic violence and harmful practices toward women, such as female genital cutting and bride burning.

How girls and women have fared since Beijing Advances in girls' education worldwide have been a success story in development. According to UNESCO, 96 girls were enrolled in primary school for every 100 boys in 2008, up from 84 girls per 100 boys in 1995. The ratio for secondary school is close behind, at 95 girls to 100 boys in 2008. By 2005, nearly two-thirds of countries had closed the gap between girls' and boys' school enrollments. Girls still lag behind boys in university-level education worldwide, but the gap is closing over time.

There is progress, but girls still lag far behind boys in countries where overall school enrollments are low, as in much of sub-Saharan Africa and Western and Southern Asia. In sub-Saharan Africa, just 39 percent of girls were enrolled in lower secondary school in 2009, according to UNESCO. UNESCO also reports that in Somalia half as many girls were enrolled in school as boys: 23 percent of girls compared to 42 percent of boys in 2008. Much work remains to be done.

At the other end of the spectrum, in countries with high levels of school enrollment, girls often fare better than boys. In much of Latin America, Europe, East Asia and in the United States, girls' enrollments in secondary and higher education have surpassed those of their male peers, demonstrating what girls and women can achieve once the barriers to education have been overcome.

Still, women account for two-thirds of the world's illiterate adults, because older women are less likely to have attended school than their younger counterparts. They are also much more likely to be illiterate if they are poor and live in rural areas. Literacy programs and continuing education exist, but the efforts are not systematically reported across countries. In addition, girls and women are disadvantaged when it comes to technical and vocational education, in fields such as science and technology that have long been dominated by men.

## What can we learn from successful efforts?

Many gains in women's education can be attributed to special interventions such as the elimination of school fees, scholarships, community schools for girls and the training of women teachers. Such targeted efforts have translated into higher girls' school enrollments in countries as diverse as Bangladesh, Yemen, Morocco, Uganda and Brazil. Political commitment is essential for raising the profile of the issue and increasing girls' access to schooling. Mexico pioneered a major social program—now replicated in impoverished communities in the United States and other countries—that pays families to keep their children, particularly girls, in school.

Because the gender gap is wider at higher levels of education, it will not be enough for girls to merely sign up for school; they need to stay in school. Governments, educators and communities must address issues such as gender stereotypes that reinforce women's lower status, poor school quality, and early marriage and childbearing, which often cut short women's education. Also, the mismatch between education and the skills needed for today's workforce must be corrected. These steps may ensure that girls reap the greatest benefits from education. Countries that are committed to gender equality will not only see better report cards in education, they'll be healthier and wealthier as well.

# 10

## Girls Are Outperforming Boys in School

### The Economist

*The* Economist *is a London-based weekly news magazine supporting a philosophy of classical and economic liberalism.*

*In many developed countries in the world, such as the United States, Australia, Sweden, and the United Kingdom, girls are surpassing boys in educational achievement. Girls read better and are catching up to boys in achievement in math. Women are attending university at higher rates than men and earning more degrees. Some research finds that girls read more for pleasure than boys and spend longer doing homework. Some experts contend that girls get better grades in school because then tend to be quieter and more docile. They also claim that girls are favored by the mostly female teaching staffs. These educational gains are not narrowing the pay gap between men and women.*

I t's all to do with their brains and bodies and chemicals," says Sir Anthony Seldon, the master of Wellington College, a posh English boarding school. "There's a mentality that it's not cool for them to perform, that it's not cool to be smart," suggests Ivan Yip, principal of the Bronx Leadership Academy in New York. One school charges £25,000 ($38,000) a year and has a scuba-diving club; the other serves subsidised lunches to most of its pupils, a quarter of whom have special needs. Yet both are grappling with the same problem: teenage boys are being left behind by girls.

"The Weaker Sex," The *Economist*, March 7, 2015. Reprinted by permission.

It is a problem that would have been unimaginable a few decades ago. Until the 1960s boys spent longer and went further in school than girls, and were more likely to graduate from university. Now, across the rich world and in a growing number of poor countries, the balance has tilted the other way. Policymakers who once fretted about girls' lack of confidence in science now spend their time dangling copies of "Harry Potter" before surly boys. Sweden has commissioned research into its "boy crisis." Australia has devised a reading programme called "Boys, Blokes, Books & Bytes." In just a couple of generations, one gender gap has closed, only for another to open up.

The reversal is laid out in a report published on March 5th by the OECD, a Paris-based rich-country think-tank. Boys' dominance just about endures in maths: at age 15 they are, on average, the equivalent of three months' schooling ahead of girls. In science the results are fairly even. But in reading, where girls have been ahead for some time, a gulf has appeared. In all 64 countries and economies in the study, girls outperform boys. The average gap is equivalent to an extra year of schooling.

## xx > xy?

The OECD deems literacy to be the most important skill that it assesses, since further learning depends on it. Sure enough, teenage boys are 50% more likely than girls to fail to achieve basic proficiency in any of maths, reading and science. Youngsters in this group, with nothing to build on or shine at, are prone to drop out of school altogether.

To see why boys and girls fare so differently in the classroom, first look at what they do outside it. The average 15-year-old girl devotes five-and-a-half hours a week to homework, an hour more than the average boy, who spends more time playing video games and trawling the internet. Three-quarters of girls read for pleasure, compared with little more than half of boys. Reading rates are falling everywhere as screens draw eyes from pages, but boys are giving up faster. The OECD found that, among boys who do as much homework as the average girl, the gender gap in reading fell by nearly a quarter.

Once in the classroom, boys long to be out of it. They are twice as likely as girls to report that school is a "waste of time," and more often turn up late. Just as teachers used to struggle to persuade girls that science is not only for men, the OECD now urges parents and policymakers to steer boys away from a version of masculinity that ignores academic achievement. "There are different pressures on boys," says Mr Yip. "Unfortunately there's a tendency where they try to live up to certain expectations in terms of [bad] behaviour."

Boys' disdain for school might have been less irrational when there were plenty of jobs for uneducated men. But those days have long gone. It may be that a bit of swagger helps in maths, where confidence plays a part in boys' lead (though it sometimes extends to delusion: 12% of boys told the OECD that they were familiar with the mathematical concept of "subjunctive scaling," a red herring that fooled only 7% of girls). But their lack of self-discipline drives teachers crazy.

Perhaps because they can be so insufferable, teenage boys are often marked down. The OECD found that boys did much better in its anonymised tests than in teacher assessments. The gap with girls in reading was a third smaller, and the gap in maths—where boys were already ahead—opened up further. In another finding that suggests a lack of even-handedness among teachers, boys are more likely than girls to be forced to repeat a year, even when they are of equal ability.

What is behind this discrimination? One possibility is that teachers mark up students who are polite, eager and stay out of fights, all attributes that are more common among girls. In some countries, academic points can even be docked for bad behaviour. Another is that women, who make up eight out of ten primary-school teachers and nearly seven in ten lower-secondary teachers, favour their own sex, just as male bosses have been shown to favour male underlings. In a few places sexism is enshrined in law: Singapore still canes boys, while sparing girls the rod.

Some countries provide an environment in which boys can do better. In Latin America the gender gap in reading is relatively small, with boys in Chile, Colombia, Mexico and Peru trailing girls less than they do elsewhere. Awkwardly, however, this nearly always comes with a wider gender gap in maths, in favour of boys. The reverse is true, too: Iceland, Norway and Sweden, which have got girls up to parity with boys in maths, struggle with uncomfortably wide gender gaps in reading. Since 2003, the last occasion when the OECD did a big study, boys in a few countries have caught up in reading and girls in several others have significantly narrowed the gap in maths. No country has managed both.

## Onwards and Upwards

Girls' educational dominance persists after school. Until a few decades ago men were in a clear majority at university almost everywhere, particularly in advanced courses and in science and engineering. But as higher education has boomed worldwide, women's enrolment has increased almost twice as fast as men's. In the OECD women now make up 56% of students enrolled, up from 46% in 1985. By 2025 that may rise to 58%.

Even in the handful of OECD countries where women are in the minority on campus, their numbers are creeping up. Meanwhile several, including America, Britain and parts of Scandinavia, have 50% more women than men on campus. Numbers in many of America's elite private colleges are more evenly balanced. It is widely believed that their opaque admissions criteria are relaxed for men.

The feminisation of higher education was so gradual that for a long time it passed unremarked. According to Stephan Vincent-Lancrin of the OECD, when in 2008 it published a report pointing out just how far it had gone, people "couldn't believe it."

Women who go to university are more likely than their male peers to graduate, and typically get better grades. But men and women tend to study different subjects, with many women choosing courses in education, health, arts and the humanities, whereas men take up computing, engineering and the exact sciences. In mathematics women are drawing level; in the life sciences, social sciences, business and law they have moved ahead.

Social change has done more to encourage women to enter higher education than any deliberate policy. The Pill and a decline in the average number of children, together with later marriage and childbearing, have made it easier for married women to join the workforce. As more women went out to work, discrimination became less sharp. Girls saw the point of study once they were expected to have careers. Rising divorce rates underlined the importance of being able to provide for yourself. These days girls nearly everywhere seem more ambitious than boys, both academically and in their careers. It is hard to believe that in 1900-50 about half of jobs in America were barred to married women.

So are women now on their way to becoming the dominant sex? Hanna Rosin's book, "The End of Men and the Rise of Women", published in 2012, argues that in America, at least, women are ahead not only educationally but increasingly also professionally and socially. Policymakers in many countries worry about the prospect of a growing underclass of ill-educated men. That should worry women, too: in the past they have typically married men in their own social group or above. If there are too few of those, many women will have to marry down or not at all.

According to the OECD, the return on investment in a degree is higher for women than for men in many countries, though not all. In America PayScale, a company that crunches incomes data, found that the return on investment in a college degree for women was lower than or at best the same as for men. Although women as a group are now better qualified, they earn about three-quarters as much as men. A big reason is the choice of subject: education, the humanities and social work pay less than engineering or computer science. But academic research shows that women attach less importance than men to the graduate pay premium, suggesting that a high financial return is not the main reason for their further education.

At the highest levels of business and the professions, women remain notably scarce. In a reversal of the pattern at school, the anonymous and therefore gender-blind essays and exams at university protect female students from bias. But in the workplace, says Elisabeth Kelan of Britain's Cranfield School of Management, "traditional patterns assert themselves in miraculous ways." Men and women join the medical and legal professions in roughly equal numbers, but 10-15 years later many women have chosen unambitious career paths or dropped out to spend time with their children. Meanwhile men are rising through the ranks as qualifications gained long ago fade in importance and personality, ambition and experience come to matter more.

## The Last Bastion

For a long time it was said that since women had historically been underrepresented in university and work, it would take time to fill the pipeline from which senior appointments were made. But after 40 years of making up the majority of graduates in some countries, that argument is wearing thin. According to Claudia Goldin, an economics professor at Harvard, the "last chapter" in the story of women's rise—equal pay and access to the best jobs—will not come without big structural changes.

In a recent paper in the *American Economic Review* Ms Goldin found that the difference between the hourly earnings of highly qualified men and their female peers grows hugely in the first 10-15 years of working life, largely because of a big premium in some highly paid jobs on putting in long days and being constantly on call. On the whole men find it easier than women to work in this way. Where such jobs are common, for example in business and the law, the gender pay gap remains wide and even short spells out of the workforce are severely penalised, meaning that motherhood can exact a heavy price. Where pay is roughly proportional to hours worked, as in pharmacy, it is low.

There will always be jobs where flexibility is not an option, says Ms Goldin: those of CEOs, trial lawyers, surgeons, some bankers and senior politicians come to mind. In many others, pay does not need to depend on being available all hours—and well-educated men who want a life outside work would benefit from change, too. But the new gender gap is at the other end of the pay spectrum. And it is not women who are suffering, but unskilled men.

# 11

## Female Infanticide Is Leading to a World of "Missing Women"

*Manisha Sharma*

*Dr. Manisha Sharma is a fiction writer, a practice-led researcher, and a poet. A founder of the initiative Gendered Arrangements, her current trans-disciplinary project focuses on the vanishing girls of India in an arresting book manuscript, art, and sound installation. The Vanishing has run nationally and internationally at universities and art galleries. Her work has been published in* Design Observer, *the* Lancet Global Health, *and the* Socjounal. *She has also presented her work at the White House. Her research has been featured in the* Stanford Social Innovation Review. *Recently, poems from The Vanishing have been published in the* Saturday Poetry Series, TAB, A Journal of Poetry and Poetics, New Asian Writing, *the* Bombay Review, *and elsewhere. More about the project, collaborators, and her work is at www.genderedarrangements.com.*

*A cultural preference for male children in many parts of the world is producing gender inequalities. In countries such as China, the Republic of Korea, and India, women are using ultrasound technology to determine the sex of a fetus so that a pregnancy can be terminated if the fetus is female. A 2011 population census in India revealed that there were 914 girls per 1000 boys between the ages of 0 and 6. The imbalance is more pronounced in impoverished rural communities.*

"Killing the little girls of the world – the lingering problem of female infanticide" by Dr. Manisha Sharma. First published in The Socjournal on June 24, 2013. Reprinted by permission.

*Legislation, awareness campaigns, and education are possible solutions to eradicate the problem of female feticide.*

For 50 years, from 1960-2011, fewer and fewer girls were allowed to be born in India. This situation, what I refer to as gendered arrangement, is old and commonly misunderstood. In India, there are "about 7.1 million fewer girls than boys aged 0-6 years." This is due to "prenatal sex determination with subsequent selective abortion of female fetuses" (Jha et.al, 2011). Data from the 2011 population census, provided by the Office of the Registrar General and Census Commissioner of India, Ministry of Home Affairs, also proves this. There are 914 girls per 1000 boys between the ages of 0 and 6. Future estimates paint a grim picture of the imbalanced demographic slide, the effects of which, research estimates, will spill beyond India.

In 1990, Nobel Laureate and economist Amartya Sen alerted the world to the phenomenon of "missing women." He said that more than 100 million women were missing from the world, which challenged the commonly held belief that women make up fifty percent of the world's population. Such a view is a generalization of the fact that there is a relatively higher number of women compared to men in Europe and North America. For a majority of the world, however, and especially in South Asia, the gender ratio favors men over women (Sen, 1990). Women in these parts of the world are considered "missing" in the sense that they aren't allowed to be born.

## Worldview

The issue of "endangered sex" is not limited to India. Cultural preference for boys extends to both China and the Republic of Korea as well, countries that have also had a history of being predominantly male; and although the Republic of Korea has been successful in reversing the gender imbalance, China continues to have a female deficit, which research says has become worse due to their one-child policy. A United Nations Population Fund report on skewed gender ratios states that in the Republic of Korea, "the imbalance could not have developed in the 1980s without modern technology, coupled with son preference and declining fertility . . . More research is needed to prove that the decrease in sex selection in Korea has been mainly due to increase in daughter preference, policy changes and shifts in socio cultural norms" (UNFPA Report, 2011).

## Historical Perspective

Girls have been eliminated in India for centuries. In the past getting rid of girls was harder and was accomplished after birth by strangling the infant girl, also known as female infanticide. During British rule over India in the 19th century, however, female infanticide was recognized as a social evil and was outlawed by the Female Infanticide Prevention Act of 1870 (Wikipedia). There have also been instances where sex of the fetus is determined before birth and the pregnant woman is beaten with blows to her stomach so that the female fetus doesn't survive (www.satyamevjayate.in).

## Current Status

For the first time in 64 years (1947-2011), the number of girls (0-6 years) in India has dropped down to 914 per 1000 boys (2011 Population Census of India). Researchers suggest that in India "there are about 400,000 sex selective abortions per year" (Skewed Sex Ratios at Birth, UNFPA, 2012), which is roughly equal to the entire estimated population of Oakland, California in 2012 (US Census Bureau). This fact relates to the more recent development in India, which is to eliminate girls even before birth.

This latest phenomenon became possible primarily through the misuse of ultrasound technology. Ultrasound technology was a major breakthrough in medical imaging in the 1980's and it also led to major developments in obstetrics and gynecology. It was intended to expedite the process of fixing issues by allowing doctors to visualize the fetus and detect abnormalities, including severe neurological disorders. Certain fetal abnormalities do not surface entirely until later in pregnancy, primarily between late first trimester and early second trimester. In such situations when fetal abnormalities can potentially threaten the life of a pregnant patient or the developing fetus, the patient may decide to abort the pregnancy. Feticide is one of the procedures used to terminate such a pregnancy. In medical literature, the term is used neutrally "as if it were unproblematic" (Graham, Robson, Rankin, 2007).

In India, the use of ultrasound has become something more precarious than a technique used to perform neutral feticides. It is largely used to determine the sex of a fetus so that the pregnancy can be terminated if the fetus is female. In academic discussions, "sex selective abortion" is a term used to refer to the abortion of a female fetus. "UNICEF reported that 43 million of the estimated 100 million women worldwide who would have been born if not for extraneous circumstances, including gender-specific abortion, would have been Indian" (Frontline PBS, 2007). So, about half of the missing female population is from India, a country that is roughly one-third the size of the United States but that has three times as many people.

## Misconceptions

The population census of India, conducted every 10 years, is the most reliable form of data on gender percentages in the country. The most current population census of 2011 has helped disprove some popular research-based perceptions about sex selective abortions.

## Son Preference

Preference for sons over daughters is cited as the number one reason for sex selective abortions in India. "One reason for desiring sons, common to all the patrilineal societies of the world, is the transmission of family name and property" (May & Herr, Populations Studies, 1968). It is expected that marrying a son will extend the family lineage. "May you be the mother of 100 sons" is still a common blessing for a pregnant woman. According to the

Hindu religion, a son or a male relative must fulfill the last rites for a parent. Most people think it worthwhile to spend money on a boy who is expected to contribute to the family even after marriage, both financially and emotionally, by supporting aging parents.

Girls are primarily considered a liability until they are married off. Spending money on educating a girl is equated to investing in a venture that has already failed. "Other's Wealth" is an adjective that is used for a daughter. No matter how much a parent or family spends on educating their daughter, most Hindu parents will not even touch the money a daughter earns whether it is before or after she marries. Instances of dowry, which is given by the bride's family to the groom's, only increase the burden of having a girl.

How can preferring a son be the sole reason for fewer and fewer girls in India, when girls have been consistently declining among all religiously affiliated and southern Indian states with a matrilineal society?

## Technology

The introduction of ultrasound technology in India is also blamed for the rapid elimination of females in India. Though sex selective abortions rose steeply after the introduction of ultrasound in India in the 1980s, it is not technology but its misuse that is responsible for the fewer number of females.

"The problem is that when it comes to sex determination, doctor and patient go hand-in-hand. Patients have to undergo ultrasound for many other medical conditions and it is difficult to find if it is for sex determination or not. One of the two stakeholders  either the patient or the doctor—needs to feel they are doing the wrong thing by looking for the unborn child's sex" (Singh, TNN 2011).

## Socioeconomic

Another common misconception is that poverty, dowry, rural Indians and poor economic status is responsible for the elimination of girls in India. In a 2000 study, Shelly Clarke concludes that "son preference is not distributed randomly, but is found to be greater among the socially and economically disadvantaged, that is uneducated, scheduled castes, rural Muslims and Hindus and non-southern states" (Sex Ratio at Birth, UNFPA, 28), while it is a fact that India's economy continued to grow even as the world's economy was "fairly uneven and uncertain" (Singh, IMF).

## Illiteracy & Ignorance

Lack of literacy and ignorance is often cited as reasons for the declining number of girls in India. Based on that logic, an improvement in the national literacy rates should reflect an improvement in the sex ratio. According to the 2011 census, all 35 states and union territories of India reported an improvement in literacy rates from 2001. 74 percent of the total Indian population, 7 years and older, is literate while only 26 percent still remains illiterate. Females, who are less in number than males, outnumber males in literacy rates by roughly 4 percent.

## Urban vs Rural

It is often believed that more rural than urban Indians opt for sex selection. Contrary to this belief, the 2011 census showed that there are fewer girls in cities (902 per 1000 boys, aged 0-6) than in villages (919 per 1000 boys, aged 0-6). Media reports in India have quoted the Census Commissioner, C. Chandramouli saying that, "It's a matter of grave concern that educated people in cities, who are better off, are opting for sex determination tests" (Singh, TNN 2011). This statistic is consistent with the conclusions drawn after the 2001 census: "The decline in urban sex ratio was more than twice that is [sic] seen in rural areas" (George, 2002; UNFPA, 31).

## North vs South

It is said the phenomenon of sex selective abortions was regional, limited to only a few North Indian states, but today more than 90% of India, i.e. 27 out of the 35 states and union territories, has fewer girls than boys (2011 population census, India). This includes some southern states that were not considered to have a deficit in girls. Previous research is not only conflicting but has been proved wrong. For example a researcher named Arokiasamy concluded in 2005 that "the rise in sex ratio at birth was steeper in the northern region while the western and eastern regions showed moderate rise [sic]" (Declining Sex Ratio in India, 21-22). The southern state of Kerala, which has the highest number of literate females in the entire country, reported a decline in the number of girls in 2001 and again in 2011, whereas Arnold's research study published in 1998 says that "Kerala was the only state that did not exhibit son preference at any parity."

## Abortion or Pro-Choice

Mostly in the west, the discourse on sex selective abortion is often seen in the same light as abortions. The argument is that a ban on sex selective abortions is taking away the choice and right of a female to control her own body, whereas for women who want to know the sex of their fetus, "it is assumed that she does so under compulsion from the family" (Gupta, Skewed Sex Ratios at Birth, UNFPA, 14). Sex selection in India is not about the choices or rights of women, in fact, in India, "sex selection is not about abortion, its [sic] about sex determination" (Vemuri, UNFPA). "The 1972 Medical Termination of Pregnancy Act in India legalized abortion in order to reduce the incidence of illegal abortions" (Legalization of abortion in India, Gupta, Pande). These misconceptions only confuse and dwarf the issue of sex selection.

It is important to realize that sex selective abortion is an Indian issue that is already causing irreparable consequences and that what is true in one culture cannot be seen as a solution for another. A majority of westerners and feminists, including Indian, view the issue simply in terms of rights and choices, but if there are no women, whose rights and choices will we talk about. The current situation is so bad that often people hesitate to talk about sex selection for fear of being perceived as belonging to the abortion or pro-choice debates. None of these situations are helping to resolve the shortage of girls in India.

## Laws vs Social Outlook

"In order to prohibit sex selection and prevent misuse of technology for preconception and prenatal sex determination, the Government of India enacted the Pre-conception and Pre-natal Diagnostics Techniques (Prohibition of Sex Selection) Act, 1994 (PCPNDTAct)" (Towards a Stronger Implementation of the PCPNDT Act, Govt. of India & UNFPA, 2012).

Since then, the act has been amended in 2003. Despite these laws, fewer and fewer girls are born in India, which has been "attributed to the introduction and proliferation of modern technology such as ultrasound that enables sex determination, thereby reinforcing societal mindsets for son preference (1). "It has been challenging to enforce the law. Effective implementation of this significant social legislation requires commitment to the ideal of gender equality and entails capacity building of all stakeholders involved in implementation of the PCPNDT Act" (1).

How do you make sure that following an ultrasound the sex of a fetus is not seen and reported to the patient? Here, the decision becomes an ethical one. The issue of sex selection is so complicated, but more than the issue itself, its interpretation is what makes the problem complex.

## The Reality

Since sex selective abortions have increased throughout India, there is no one reason that fits all. Despite the enactment of prohibitory laws intended to protect unborn girls, the truth is that in India selective abortion of female fetuses is a very real problem, one that has spread like an epidemic, engulfing the entire country. The archives of local and national newspapers have reported instances of female fetuses, ranging from a few weeks to 15-18 weeks, found floating in bodies of water, dumped in sewers, or abandoned in Medical College campuses in Udaipur, Jaipur, Pali and other cities of Rajasthan (The Tribune, 2006).

## The Way Ahead

Decreasing number of females in India is a problem that people intellectually understand, but when it comes to personal issues, they often go against their own logic. How do you resolve such a complex problem? Many special groups, activists, media and government organizations, as well as non-governmental organizations (NGOs), are trying to address the issue in their own way, and yet there is a disconnect when it comes to stakeholders, their stories, and the interaction among these different groups. Moreover, often the way various groups address the issue is in conflict with each other, except the fact that the number of girls is decreasing. Activists and social workers talk about the reality they see on the ground, which scholars, researchers and policy makers consider as "emotionally charged."

If there is a problem, there has to be a solution too, but where does the solution come from? The impact of the female feticide requires that the issue be addressed by multiple agencies in various mediums, since there are various stakeholders here, and not everyone understands a similar language. Keeping the wide cross section of society in mind, awareness campaigns need to be catered to specific audience, for example the issue should be addressed through the medium of art, music, theater, informal conversations, writing, and so forth. It is important to hear people's stories and narratives, out of which a solution may emerge. Acknowledging the positive in society is another way. Simplifying the issue itself is a big problem. Scholars need to step out of their ivory tower and interact with people in a language that they can understand.

In an attempt to simplify and understand the problem, I am working on a digital and visual rhetoric of videos and infographs: a combination of words and visuals in a poster. If there is a problem, a solution must be there.

# *References*

Census of India: Provisional Population Totals 2011: India: Census 2011. (2011). doi: http://censusindia.gov.in/2011-prov-results/data_files/india/pov_popu_total_presentation_2011.pdf

Graham, Ruth H., Rankin, Judith M, Robson, Stephen C (2008). "Understanding feticide: An analytic review. *Social Science and Medicine*, 66 (289–300)

Gupta, O.P., Pandey, N.L. Legalization of Abortion in India, US National Library of Medicine, *National Institutes of Health*. doi: http://www.ncbi.nlm.nih.gov/pubmed/12336413

Prabhat Jha et. al. (2011). doi: http://cghr.org/wordpress/wp-content/uploads/Trends-in-selective-abortions-of-girls-in-India-2011.pdf

May DA, Herr DM (1968). Son survivorship motivation and family size in India: A computer simulation. *Population Studies*. doi: http://www.ncbi.nlm.nih.gov/pubmed/22091610

Sen, Amartya (1990). More Than 100 Million Women are Missing. *The New York Review of Books*. doi:http://www.nybooks.com/articles/archives/1990/dec/20/more-than-100-million-women-are-missing/?pagination=false

Singh, Anoop. Urban India pips is sex selection, http://blog-imfdirect.imf.org/2011/10/25/india-linked-or-de-linked-from-the-global-economy/

United States Census Bureau. doi: http://quickfacts.census.gov/qfd/states/06/0653000.html

UNFPA. Report of the International Workshop on Skewed Sex Ratios at Birth: Addressing the Issue and the Way Forward. doi: http://www.unfpa.org/webdav/site/global/shared/documents/publications/2012/Report_SexRatios_2012.pdf

Vemuri, Anuradha.(2012). Presentations made by Resource Persons at the PNDT Workshop. UNFPA. doi: http://india.unfpa.org/drive/PresentationmadeatthePNDTWorkshop.pdf

UNFPA India, Reports. (2012) Towards a Stronger Implementation of the Pre-Conception and Pre-Natal Diagnostic Techniques (PCPNDT) Act. doi: http://india.unfpa.org/drive/PCNDTworkshop_report19final.pdf

"2 more female foetuses found," Tribune, last updated September 4, 2006, http://www.tribuneindia.com/2006/20060905/nation.htm#16.

# 12

# Women Are Using Social Media to Combat Violence Against Women in Elections

*Gabrielle Bardall*

*Gabrielle Bardall is an academic and an electoral assistance expert with a decade of experience supporting electoral processes in transitional states. She has worked with UN Women, UNDP, the International Foundation for Electoral Systems, Democracy Reporting International, the Carter Center, and other organizations to educate, advise, and advocate on issues of women's political participation in over twenty-five countries.*

*Information and communication technologies (ICTs) such as social media sites have been used to perpetrate a range of violent acts toward women in elections (VAWE) in many countries. Because of their anonymity, low cost, and ubiquitous presence, sites such as Twitter have been used to intimidate, harass, threaten, humiliate, and incite physical and psychological attacks on women who run for office. However, women are fighting back using the same technologies. They are able to collect data, raise awareness, and use social media sites as tools for advocacy, empowerment, and activism.*

## Abstract

The rising influence of new information and communication technologies (ICTs) has paralleled the rapid development of women's political participation worldwide. For women entering

"Gender-Specific Election Violence: The Role of Information and Communication Technologies," Gabrielle Bardall, April 22, 2013, http://www.stabilityjournal.org/articles/10.5334/sta.cs/. Licensed under CC BY 4.0 International.

political life or holding public positions, new ICTs are frequently used as tools of gender-specific electoral and political violence. There is evidence of ICTs being used to perpetrate a broad range of violent acts against women during elections, especially acts inflicting fear and psychological harm. Specific characteristics of ICTs are particularly adapted to misuse in this manner. Despite these significant challenges, ICTs also offer groundbreaking solutions for preventing and mitigating violence against women in elections (VAWE). Notably, ICTs combat VAWE through monitoring and documenting violence, via education and awareness-raising platforms and through empowerment and advocacy initiatives.

## The Specific Challenge of Violence Against Women in Elections

Substantial gains have been made worldwide in enhancing women's participation in public life in the past two decades. In 1995, women comprised at least 30 per cent of parliamentarians in only five countries (2 per cent of the total), while today thirty-one states have reached that threshold.[1] Constitutional revisions and electoral reform have enfranchised women and facilitated their political participation by entrenching their rights, offering incentives and/ or imposing sanctions on political parties and other public bodies to protect against gender-specific threats. Nonetheless, women generally remain acutely under-represented in parliaments (only 21.2 per cent of parliamentarians worldwide are women) and face deep-rooted obstacles to participation as voters and in other civil and public roles. Barriers range from inadequate or nonexistent legal protections, traditional cultural stereotypes and gender roles, lack of access to resources and civic education and generally lower levels of self-confidence in pursuing public office. Of all of these barriers, gender-specific election violence is perhaps the most insidious, affecting and compounding other obstacles.

Women's experience of election violence is fundamentally different from that of men (Bardall 2010a). Firstly, women are far more likely to be victims of election violence (defined as "any harm, or threat of harm, to any persons or property involved in the election process, or the election process itself, during the election period" (Kammerud 2011) than perpetrators (Bardall 2010a). Violence against women in elections (VAWE) refers to any random or conspiratorial act to discourage, suppress, or prevent women from exercising their electoral rights. This includes women's participation as voters, candidates, party supporters, election workers, observers, journalists, or public officials (UNDP forthcoming). VAWE may take place in both public and private spheres. Like other common forms of election violence, VAWE is commonly perpetrated by political opponents and party militants; however it may also be perpetrated by family members, domestic partners, religious leaders and the media.

Incidents of VAWE can be distinguished by their various forms and frequencies. Although VAWE may comprise physical, sexual or economic acts of aggression, psychological attacks are by far the most pervasive form of VAWE. Indeed, research has found that women experience only one-third as many direct physical attacks as men but are three times as likely to experience psychological violence (Bardall 2010a). Psychological violence is an "informal means of control [and] includes systematic ridicule, ostracism, shame, sarcasm, criticism, disapproval, exclusion and discrimination" (Bardall 2010a). Coupled with threats of physical and sexual violence, these forms of violence degrade, demoralize and shame their victims. These psychological forms of election violence are the most devastating to women. And, increasingly, they are orchestrated through the instruments of social media.

## Social Media as Implements of Violence Against Women in Elections

The UN estimates that 95 per cent of aggressive behavior, harassment, abusive language and denigrating images in online spaces are aimed at women, most often by a current or former partner (UNGA 2006). As women's participation in politics grows despite ongoing legal barriers and cultural resistance, their vulnerability to election violence increases proportionately, including in online spaces and via ICTs. Karen Banks noted over ten years ago that "[t]he internet is not creating new forms of crimes against women [...], but it is creating new ways and means for crimes to be perpetrated" (Banks 2001: 147–173) However, the implications of these new ways and means on women's political participation is rarely discussed. In particular, the Internet and other social media and ICTs have proven to be uniquely dangerous instruments in perpetrating election violence against women because of the relative importance of psychological violence in women's political experience.

ICTs may be used directly as a tool of intimidation by threatening or inciting physical violence against women candidates, voters or representatives. Such cyber-harassment or intimidation may include sending abusive, threatening or obscene emails from one person to another with explicit threats of physical and/or sexual violence. It may involve electronic sabotage in the form of extensive spam and damaging viruses, impersonating the victim online and sending abusive emails or fraudulent spams, blog-posts, Tweets and other online communications in the victim's name or subscribing victims to unwanted email lists resulting in hundreds of unwanted messages daily (Ellison and Akdeniz 1998).

Cyber-harassment can result in serious harm to the victim, as in the 1996 case of Cynthia Armistead, an American woman who received thousands of offensive messages and threats after her stalker published false online advertisements offering her services as a prostitute and providing her home address and personal telephone number (Bocij 2004). More innovative and sophisticated forms of ICT-based attacks on women have been documented and include the use of "spy software" (spyware enables abusers to have access to all keystrokes made on the computer, including all email correspondence, web surfing and internet communication); the use of wireless technology to monitor private conversations; hacking; saved "cookies" and browser histories; email tampering and interception; visual surveillance and geographic tracking via

Global Positioning System (GPS) software (Southworth et al. 2007). These ICT-based attacks have an overwhelming impact on women's private and professional lives. Indeed, some surveys estimate that over 80 per cent of victims in cyber-stalking[2] incidents are women.[3]

The use of these and other forms of ICT-based violence has been documented in cases of VAWE. During the post-election violence in Kenya in 2008–09, tribal-based political partisans sent SMS messages to women in opposing tribal-based political groups, threatening bodily harm, rape and even death (Muthoni; Wanyeki). In an American web-based video game promoted by The Hillary Project, players score points when they slap former US secretary of state and potential presidential candidate, Hillary Clinton, each time she speaks.[4] Graphically violent Tweets were used to make rape and murder threats against British Member of Parliament Stella Creasy and other prominent British women at a rate of up to 50 threats per hour, over the course of 12 hours following their support of a feminist issue (Döing 2013). During the 2008 US presidential campaign, computer hackers broke into the private email account of vice-presidential candidate Sarah Palin and posted some of her messages and many of her contacts online (Falcone 2008).

Beyond these evident misuses of the medium, a number of the specific qualities of social media make them peculiarly suited to inflicting psychological violence on women in public life. Their disproportionate impact on women stems in large part from women's unique vulnerability to attacks on the basis of morality. By breaking into a traditionally masculine field that is frequently associated with rough behavior and corruption, women are exposed to sexualized and/or morally degrading criticism. Derogatory accusations of being a prostitute, a lesbian or otherwise sinful and/or sexually deviant are commonly leveled against women running for office in many countries. These moral attacks often carry much greater social costs for women than for men because of the implications they may have on the victim's children or because of the existence of double standards as far as what constitutes "moral behavior" for male and female politicians (i.e., branding mommy "a whore" may imply she is unfit for office while calling daddy "a philanderer" may not be considered as serious an offence, or may even infer virility and strength). The specific nature of social media plays to these imbalances and exacerbates attacks on women in public life in several ways.

Firstly, the nature of messaging in social media facilitates ridicule, shaming and other psychological forms of VAWE. The most effective social media messages are generally short (in the case of Twitter, limited to 140 characters), written in simple language and often humorous.[5] A study of media coverage of Hillary Clinton and Sarah Palin's 2008 political campaigns in the US found that the crudest attacks were found online, including over 500 YouTube videos under the search "Hillary" and "bitch" and multiple Facebook groups with obscene or sexist names, including the most popular (41,025 followers in March 2008) "Hillary Clinton: Stop running for president and make me a sandwich" (Jamieson and Dunn 2008). Crude and sensational messages circulate widely without the legal or professional ethical requirements of traditional media to ensure accuracy, check sources and rectify errors. With extremely low barriers to entry, social media users may engage in character assassination at virtually no cost and with little personal consequence.

Social media also facilitates attacks on women's ethics and morality through the ubiquitous presence of images. The use of stereotypical or demeaning images and photos to sexualize, emotionalize and trivialize women poses a strong disincentive for women considering running for office, and may even pose a direct threat to their personal safety (Blackman-Woods 2013). Women MPs in many countries report feeling compelled to be hyper-conscious about their appearance and physical posture in public, due to the ubiquity of cell phone cameras.[6] Candid shots taken at unguarded moments and immediately posted and disseminated online have a degrading and intimidating impact on women candidates and MPs. Exacerbating the issue, the ease of programs such as Photoshop allows perpetrators to modify snapshots or create entirely new images designed to denigrate, compromise or shame their victim. In the case of female politicians, this is commonly manifested through sexually suggestive or demeaning images. With YouTube, videography is often matched with music and can be used to promote violence towards women in politics, for example in a YouTube music video during the 2008 US campaign that flashed photos of Hillary Clinton during debates as the lyric "I'll beat that bitch with a hit" was repeated (Jamieson and Dunn 2008). This form of violence, known as malicious distribution, uses technology as a tool to manipulate and distribute defamatory and/or illegal material related to the victim (Baker et al. 2013).

The speed with which information travels through social media networks and the scope of its diffusion magnify the impact of acts of VAWE (Kee 2005). Re-Tweets, shares and "Likes" spread degrading, humiliating or threatening attacks on women in politics with almost uncontrollable rapidity. The scope of online stalking and harassment are likewise amplified (Arya 2013). Available redress for this type of attack, including community censure, website moderating and legal intervention, frequently take effect only after the damage to the victim has been done. Self-policing functions of websites such as Facebook and Twitter are often weak and/or vulnerable to gender bias.[7] Interventions may interrupt or halt a behavior but less frequently correct false accusations or degrading projections. Indeed, given tight electoral deadlines, harm to a victim's public image may be difficult or impossible to correct before ballots are cast. The reach of any given message on social media is dependent on the voluntary diffusion of the message by social media users. Therefore efforts to rectify degrading depictions cannot be consistently broadcast to consumers of the original message. Finally, the speed and scope of social media attacks have a chilling effect on political aspirants, especially women entering politics for the first time. Women frequently cite the threat of widespread, rapid public attacks on personal dignity as a factor deterring women from entering politics.[8]

In contrast to many forms of ICT-based VAWE that target a woman's public image, ICTs may also cause harm by their ability to silence and bury women who otherwise seek to build a public presence for political aims. Some recent cases demonstrate explicit attacks on women's access to and visibility via ICTs. Between 2010 and 2013, Indian villages in Bihar and Uttar Pradesh states and the Priyadarshni Indira Gandhi Government College for Women in Haryana banned single (or undergraduate) women from using cell phones (single/undergraduate men were not affected). In 2004, the Saudi Arabian Ministry of Education banned women from carrying camera phones. Polls in Nigeria have registered support for banning women's use of mobile phones (APC 2013). Control over women's access to ICTs is also reported extensively as a tool of domestic violence including privacy invasion through SMS stalking, monitoring use and/or withholding permission from female family members who want to use cell phones (Madanda et al. 2009).

Media bias in coverage of female candidates tends to bury women's platforms behind excessive coverage of their appearance, personality and family, in comparison to male candidates (Bystrom 2004). Private and public media overtly limit or tolerate biased media coverage of female candidates, for example during the 2011–12 Egyptian elections when media conceded to demands from conservative parties to prohibit unveiled women candidates and broadcasters from participating in mixed-group debates. Reports of political parties limiting women candidates' access to party media resources also contribute to burying their public visibility.

Finally, violence perpetrated through social media benefits from a significant degree of legal and moral impunity. The perpetrator may feel a certain moral impunity as a result of being distanced from the victim. In social media, the perpetrator may never meet his/her victim in person and never see the impact of his/her acts, thereby dehumanizing the victim. Should he/she fear censure, the perpetrator may choose to remain anonymous, either to his/her immediate community or to general society.

A cyber-stalker or other online perpetrators can conceal his/her identity to a degree otherwise impossible in traditional violence, by using different ISPs and/or by adopting different screen names. More sophisticated perpetrators can use anonymous remailers to virtually erase their association as the source of an email or other online communication (Munyua et al. 2010).

The sense of impunity related to social media-based harassment and aggression may also be amplified because these acts lack identifiable leadership. An "incident" of VAWE on social media is different in nature from a traditional act where the perpetrator is clearly identifiable. Instead, an incident of online violence is a collective phenomenon and may involve dozens or even thousands of "perpetrators." Terrifying for the victim, this is also empowering for the authors of violence. Perpetrators may gain confidence and feel social approbation when their messages are shared, re-Tweeted or "Liked" on the Internet. Without a clear sense of direction or identification, social media users may feel diminished accountability when they promote hurtful messages through their networks.

A final reason social media-based violence can be so treacherous for women in politics is the difficulty of regulating and punishing attacks. The realm of social media is one of relative legal impunity for the authors of electoral violence against women. Legal protections defining gender-based violence and sexual crimes are lacking or entirely absent in many countries. This gap is compounded by the even greater gap existing in the realm of cybercrime in many states (Madanda et al. 2013). Common protections against ICT-based violence against women may be limited to defending against stalking and harassment through telephone calls and electronic mail (Essof 2009). Only two countries, Mexico and Bolivia, have specific legislation addressing violence against women in elections.[9] Access to justice for women is similarly challenging and, for women who do successfully bring their cases to court, favorable rulings and enforcement of criminal sentences or penalties may prove elusive.

Electoral violence perpetrated through social media channels is thus virtually impossible to limit or prosecute.

## Fighting VAWE Through Information and Communication Technologies

Information and communication technologies are also tools of empowerment for women entering politics and combatting all forms of VAWE, especially social media-based acts of VAWE. Indeed, some of the same attributes that make social media an effective implement of violence make it an effective remedy. In 1995, at the Fourth World Conference on Women, the Beijing Plan of Action called on states as well as media systems and associations and NGOs to increase the participation and access of women to expression and decision-making in and through the media and new technologies of communication. Almost twenty years after Beijing, social media is being used to combat VAWE through three main areas: 1) monitoring and documenting VAWE, 2) educating and awareness-raising and 3) empowerment and advocacy initiatives.

Monitoring and documenting gender-based violence (GBV) is notoriously challenging due to the intimate and often humiliating nature of the violence and fear of retribution. In the case of election-related GBV, these factors are compounded by the lack of awareness of the link between election violence and GBV and the perceived need of women candidates to publically "save face" by hiding their experience of violence. Yet baseline data on the presence of VAWE is vital to raising the profile of the problem, aiding its victims and identifying appropriate solutions to mitigate and prevent it in the future. ICTs are making major contributions toward overcoming some of these challenges and establishing critical documentation of the problem. Traditional sources of documentation for election monitoring and observation missions (EOMs) have expanded and are now able to more effectively monitor social media traffic thanks to the introduction of low-cost or public-domain software services such as Hootsuite, TweetReach, Klout, Social Mention and many others. As the issue of VAWE becomes more widely recognized and mainstreamed in election observation, these tools will enable EOMs to document incidents of social media-based violence and analyze their trends.

ICTs also facilitate the collection of data on acts of VAWE perpetrated "offline" (i.e., traditional acts of physical, psychological and sexual election violence). Incidents of VAWE can be easily mapped and monitored for patterns and frequencies thanks to open source software mash-ups such as Ushahidi. Ushahidi draws on crowd-sources data collected from the public at large via SMS, Twitter, Facebook, YouTube, phone calls and email. The data is transmitted to a web platform and mapped visually using publically-accessible maps such a GoogleMaps. Most critical of all, victims of violence are increasingly able to report acts of VAWE without fear of physical retribution or public shame, thanks to the anonymity of ICTs (Chaio 2011). As demonstrated in Ushahidi deployments in Egypt and in Syria, where the Ushahidi platform has been used to specifically document GBV (Harassmap), women feel empowered to speak out safely about their experience of violence when they are able to do so quickly (through their cell phones) and anonymously. Users have testified to the sense of empowerment provided by being able to securely yet publically denounce assaults on their dignity (Harassmap).

Rapid response to mitigate VAWE and early warning to prevent it are both enabled through individual ICTs and powerful mash-ups such as Ushahidi. Social media monitoring software permits rapid identification of abusive posts and Twitter "trends," enabling actors to respond quickly to limit the damage. The use of SMS messaging for documenting GBV has the added benefit of enabling instant and discreet referral services to victims via text message. In some countries, Ushahidi has been used to establish an early warning system for election violence. In 2010 in Burundi, an IFES-led coalition, Amatora Mu Mahoro, analyzed election violence trends reported via Ushahidi for early warning purposes (Bardall 2010b). Likewise, the Women's Situation Room initiative deployed in several sub-Saharan African states in recent years (UN Women

2012) has used incident reports collected via SMS, cell phones and other ICTs to provide rapid response to victims (Bardall 2010a). The use of ICTs in the Situation Rooms empower women to act as stewards of the peace. Through mobilization, mediation and multi-sector coordination, these programs reinforce this key civic role performed by women in many countries.

A final component of research and documentation is the development of online platforms to store and share knowledge on the issue of ICTs and gender violence. GenderIT.org has been the leader in this area and provides an information resource and knowledge-sharing site for gender and ICT advocates, civil society organizations and policy makers, focused on Africa, Asia-Pacific, Central Eastern Europe and Latin America. Associated with the Association for Progressive Communications (Women's Networking Support Programme), the website promotes issues paper and research exploring the intersection between the internet and violence against women, women's rights, sexuality and sexual rights.[10]

ICTs also promote the prevention and mitigation of VAWE in a second area: awareness-raising. The connection between election violence and gender-based violence is poorly understood. Trainings for women candidates and aspirants help identify the links and empower women to protect and prepare themselves from attacks by using social media tools to respond effectively. Training programs offered by non-profit organizations like the National Democratic Institute (Borovsky et al. 2010) as well as public resources to orient women aspirants[11] help women to use social media to their advantage, fight against attacks, establish a credible online image to decrease their vulnerability to attacks and enable them to quickly respond and defend themselves in case of attack.

ICTs are being used to educate women about other ICT-based risks. Specific online courses exist to promote victim safety from ICT-related violence against women. For example, Safety Net Canada (SNC) is a national initiative that addresses how technology impacts safety, privacy, accessibility, self-determination, justice and human rights for survivors of domestic and sexual violence, stalking, harassment and abuse. Online courses are also offered for service providers, anti-violence workers, law enforcement, and members of civil and criminal justice systems to educate and inform about the use of technology to stalk and harass victims.[12]

Awareness-raising also extends to the media itself, where much of the violence is perpetrated. Awareness-raising and professional standards trainings for journalists and media professionals are offered by international aid providers, such as in 2011 in Tunisia where the United Nations Development Program and the Center of Arab Woman for Training and Research organized multiple seminars, cascade trainings and debates on gender-sensitive media coverage (CAWTAR).

Digital-storytelling is another ICT-based tool being developed to respond to the challenge of VAW and which holds great promise for awareness-raising around VAWE. Bearing witness to experiences of violence promotes awareness and action, as well as providing a voice to the victims. Digital Storytelling spans a variety of digital narrative forms (web-based stories, interactive stories, hypertexts, and narrative computer games) and may use digital cameras, digital voice recorders, iMovie, Movie Maker and Final Cut Express to create 2 to 3 minute multimedia movies that combine photographs, video, animation, sound, music, text, and often a narrative voice and are published online on YouTube, Vimeo, CD/DVD and via podcast (Craig 2006). Digital storytelling has been used to support victims of gender-based violence and to promote awareness worldwide in the past decade, through the work of initiatives such as Silence Speaks, the Saartjie Baartman Centre for Women and Children (South Africa), Sonke Gender Justice Network (South Africa) and others (Roland 2006).

Finally, ICTs have made inroads in preventing and mitigating VAWE by serving as tools of advocacy, empowerment and activism. Although the anonymity provided by social media can be a benefit in addressing VAWE in some circumstances, social media's high visibility facilitates networking, mediatizing and mobilization around an otherwise private issue.

Advocacy can be targeted to respond to specific events or in support of individual candidates. For example, in response to the online game to slap Hillary Clinton, EMILY's List (an American political network that supports progressive women candidates to be elected to political office), successfully mobilized its online network to collect 20,000 signatures in 24 hours to demand political groups suspend funding to the Hillary Project and any other group advocating violence against women. While impressive in scope, the effectiveness of this type of response may rely on the woman candidate's existing support network and public profile, which, for some newcomers, may not be well established.

Beyond individual initiatives, ICT advocacy campaigns are especially effective in addressing the cross-cutting issue of VAWE. In particular, non-governmental organizations have been shown to effectively use ICTs to further initiatives, raise awareness, forge networks and exchange information on broad issues of VAW (HAMM 2001). Similar applications of ICTs in promoting women in politics have also emerged in recent years. Responses to addressing VAWE through ICTs may be identified at the intersection of these two areas.

Rutgers University's 16 Days of Activism Against Gender Violence Campaign is an international campaign that mobilizes ICT to prevent violence against women. Over 5,167 organizations in approximately 187 countries have participated in the 16 Days Campaign since its inception in 1991. Working in the context of the 16 Days, the "Take Back the Tech" campaign seeks to train ICT users in employing activism against violence against women. The stated goals of the campaign are to "raise awareness about the way ICTs are connected to violence against women; provide simple strategies on how incidences of violence against women (VAW) can be minimised online; generate discussion around the connections between ICTs and VAW in online and offline spaces, and build a community that will continue to strategise around eliminating

VAW through, and in, ICT spaces" (Take Back the Tech). The campaign draws on an extensive array of ICT and social media tools to empower women at both the personal and broader public levels. These tools include using internet platforms for advocacy, mapping attacks (hacking, blocking, deletion) of the websites of women's rights organizations, sexual rights advocates, feminist activists and bloggers, and user-friendly games to promote safety in social networks. The campaign is active in over 25 countries worldwide. Although the political dimension of VAW is not fully integrated into the campaign, Take Back the Tech is a model for ICT-based advocacy against VAW.

Perhaps the most significant embodiment of ICTs as a tool of political empowerment is through the International Knowledge Network of Women in Politics (iKNOW Politics). Women's access to global communication networks and their potential for public policy were brought to center stage during the Fourth World Conference on Women in Beijing (UN 1995). One of the outcomes of this consensus in Beijing was the creation of an online workspace designed to serve the needs of elected officials, candidates, political party leaders, researchers and other practitioners interested in advancing women in politics. Through the use of a technology-based forum, the iKnow Politics partners, UNDP, UN Women, NDI, the IPU and International IDEA, offer an interactive and multi-lingual tool that allows members and users to access resources, share expertise and create knowledge through mediated discussion forums and consolidated expert responses to queries. Today, iKnow Politics offers the most publically accessible and extensive collection of resources on the issue of VAWE, including country case studies, news, interviews, academic articles and policy papers.

## ICTs, Gender and Election Violence

Information and communication technologies have had a profound impact on the reach and shape of violence against women in elections, creating new threats and obstacles to achieving gender equality in political life. The use of ICTs in combatting election-

and political-related violence against women is only emerging today, largely because the issue of VAWE is poorly understood and recognized. One of the greatest advantages to date has been the use of ICTs to collect and document incidents of VAWE, thereby recognizing the existence of the problem and establishing baselines for progress. These innovations must come a long way yet to catch up to the threats posed by social media-based violence against women in elections. To do so, it is necessary to address the underlying dangers presented by social media—specifically, psychological forms of violence designed to attack women's dignity, morality and self-worth. Both gender and elections-rights advocates and practitioners seeking to prevent and mitigate this unique form of violence will gain by integrating the best practices from their mutual fields.

## *Notes*

[1] Inter-Parliamentary Union, www.parline.org, Reflects single and lower houses. In 1995, women comprised more than 30 per cent of seats in only Sweden, Norway, Finland, Denmark and the Netherlands. As of September 2013, thirty-one states have surpassed 30 per cent women in single or lower house seats (in descending order): Rwanda, Andorra, Cuba, Sweden, Seychelles, Senegal, Finland, South Africa, Nicaragua, Iceland, Norway, Mozambique, Denmark, Ecuador, Netherlands, Costa Rica, Timor-Leste, Belgium, Argentina, Mexico, Spain, Tanzania, Uganda, Angola, Macedonia, Grenada, Nepal, Serbia, Germany, New Zealand, Slovenia, Algeria, Zimbabwe, Italy, Guyana and Burundi.

[2] For a complete discussion of cybercrime and women, see Munyua, Mureithi and Githaiga.

[3] WHO@ is volunteer organization founded in 1997 to fight online harassment. Statistics are based on incidents reported primarily from the United States in 2012, as well as a limited number of cases in Europe. See:http://www.haltabuse.org/about/about.shtml

[4] See: http://thehillaryproject.com/games/

[5] Elections municipales au Canada: Guide à l'intention des candidates

[6] Author's interviews with women MPs and candidates, including Tunisia, July 2013; Haiti, April 2013; Nigeria, January 2013; Egypt, November – January 2011–12.

[7] See Al Jazeera, "Does Facebook have a 'violence against women' problem?" Available at http://stream.aljazeera.com/story/201305222040-0022771 and Helen Davidson, The Guardian, "Facebook locks out campaigner against images of violence against women." Available at http://www.theguardian.com/world/2013/may/31/facebook-locks-out -campaigner-women

[8] Author's interviews.

[9] Bolivia's Law against Harassment and Political Violence against Women was passed May 12, 2012. In 2013, the Mexican Senate established a definition of acts that constitute political gender violence.

[10] See www.genderit.org

[11]For example: Status of Women Canada. Federation of Canadian Municipalities. "Elections Municipales au Canada: Guide à l'intention des candidates."
[12]See: Western Education Learning Network, Center for Research & Education on Violence Against Women & Children. "Online Training to Promote Safety for ICT-Related VAW." Available at http://www.vawlearningnetwork.ca/sites/learningtoendabuse.ca.vawlearningnetwork/files/Online_Training_Promote_Safety.pdf

# Organizations to Contact

*The editors have compiled the following list of organizations concerned with the issues debated in this book. The descriptions are derived from materials provided by the organizations. All have publications or information available for interested readers. The list was compiled on the date of publication of the present volume; the information provided here may change. Be aware that many organizations take several weeks or longer to respond to inquiries, so allow as much time as possible.*

**American Association of University Women (AAUW)**
111 Sixteenth Street NW
Washington, DC 20036
(800) 326-2287
email: connect@aauw.org
website: http://www.aauw.org

The American Association of University Women (AAUW) advocates for equity and education for women and girls. AAUW members have examined and taken positions on the educational, social, economic, and political issues that concern girls and women. Its website contains background and explanations on topics such as gender equity, sex discrimination, and educational opportunities for women.

**Equal Rights Advocates (ERA)**
180 Howard Street, Suite 300
San Francisco, CA 94105
(415) 621-0672
email: info@equalrights.org
website: http://www.equalrights.org

Equal Rights Advocates is a national civil rights organization dedicated to protecting and expanding economic and educational access and opportunities for women and girls. It advocates for women's equality through public education, legislation, lobbying, and litigation. ERA provides numerous reports and fact sheets, including Know Your Rights brochure *Sex Discrimination at Work*.

**League of Women Voters of the United States (LWV)**
1730 M Street NW, Suite 1000
Washington, DC 20036-4508
(202) 429-1965
website: http://www.lwv.org

The League of Women Voters of the United States, a nonpartisan political organization, has fought since 1920 to improve systems of government and impact public policies through citizen education and advocacy. The LWV is a grassroots organization, working at the national, state, and local levels.

**National Congress of Black Women, Inc. (NCBW)**
1250 Fourth Street SW, Suite WG-1
Washington, DC 20024
(202) 678-6788
email: info@nationalcongressbw.org
website: http://nationalcongressbw.org

The NCBW supports the advancement of African American women in politics and government. The organization also engages in research on critical issues that affect the quality of life of African American women and youth. Through its Commission on Entertainment, the NCBW campaigns against the glorification of violence, misogyny, pornography, and drugs in popular entertainment. It publishes project reports on its website, including "Crusading Against Gangsta/Porno Rap."

**National Organization for Women (NOW)**
1100 H Street NW, Suite 300
Washington, DC 20005
(202) 628-8669
website: http://www.now.org

The largest organization of feminist activists in the United States, NOW has 500,000 contributing members and 550 chapters in all fifty states and the District of Columbia. Since its founding in 1966, NOW's goal has been to take action to bring about equality for all women. NOW activists do extensive electoral and lobbying work and bring lawsuits. NOW also organize mass marches, rallies, pickets, and non-violent civil disobedience.

**National Women's Law Center (NWLC)**
11 Dupont Circle NW, #800
Washington, DC 20036
(202) 588-5180
email: info@nwlc.org
website: http://www.nwlc.org

The National Women's Law Center is a not-for-profit law firm that represents women's interests in issues such as child care, education and Title IX, health care and reproductive rights, the military, the workplace, and retirement. Its website provides data regarding women's legal rights in individual states.

**Rutgers Institute for Women's Leadership**
162 Ryders Lane
New Brunswick, NJ 08901-8555
(848) 932-1463
website: http://iwl.rutgers.edu

The institute and its members are dedicated to examining leadership issues and advancing women's leadership in all arenas of public life—locally, nationally. and globally. The institute encourages scholarly and practical explorations of how institutions are structured by gender, race and ethnicity, and socioeconomic status, and promotes new understanding of women's leadership for social change. Its website provides fact sheets on a variety of issues concerning women's leadership.

**Women Impacting Public Policy (WIPP)**
PO Box 31279
San Francisco, CA 94131
(415) 434-4314
website: http://www.wipp.org

Women Impacting Public Policy is a national nonpartisan public policy organization that advocates for and on behalf of women and minorities in business in the legislative processes of our nation, creating economic opportunities and building bridges and alliances to other small business organizations.

**YWCA USA**
2025 M Street NW, Suite 550
Washington, DC 20036
(202) 467-0801
email: info@ywca.org
website: http://www.ywca.org

The YWCA is one of the oldest and largest multicultural women's organization in the world. Across the globe, the organization has more than 25 million members in 106 countries, including 2.6 million members and participants in 300 local associations in the United States. The YWCA's mission is to eliminate racism and empower women.

**Zonta International**
1211 West 22nd Street, Suite 900
Oak Brook, IL 60523
(630) 928-1400
email: zontaintl@zonta.org
website: http://www.zonta.org

Zonta International is a global organization of executives and professionals working together to advance the status of women worldwide through service and advocacy. With more than 31,000 members in 66 countries and geographic areas, members volunteer their time, talents, and support to local and international service projects as well as scholarship programs.

# Bibliography

## Books

Barbara Boxer. *The Art of Tough: Fearlessly Facing Politics and Life.* New York, NY: Hachette Book Group, 2016.

Susan J. Carroll and Richard L. Fox, eds. *Gender & Elections.* New York, NY: Cambridge University Press, 2014.

Hillary Rodham Clinton. *Hard Choices.* New York, NY: Simon & Schuster, 2014.

Julie Dolan, Melissa M. Deckman, and Michele L. Swers. *Women and Politics: Paths to Power and Political Influence.* Lanham, MA: Rowman & Littlefield, 2016.

Clair Duncanson. *Gender and Peacebuilding.* Malden, MA: Polity Press, 2016.

Linda Hirshman. *Sisters in Law: How Sandra Day O'Connor and Ruth Bader Ginsburg Went to the Supreme Court and Changed the World.* New York, NY: HarperCollins, 2015.

Mona Lena Krook and Sarah Childs., eds. *Women, Gender, and Politics: A Reader.* New York, NY: Oxford University Press, 2010.

Regina G. Lawrence and Melody Rose. *Hillary Clinton's Race for the White House: Gender Politics & the Media on the Campaign Trail.* Boulder, CO: Lynne Rienner Publishers, 2010.

Ellen R. Malcolm and Craig Unger. *When Women Win: EMILY's List and the Rise of Women in American Politics.* Boston, MA: Houghton Mifflin Harcourt Publishing, 2016.

Dorothy E. McBride and Janine A. Parry. *Women's Rights in the USA: Policy Debates and Gender Roles.* New York, NY: Routledge, 2011.

Jay Newton-Small. *Broad Influence: How Women Are Changing the Way America Works.* New York, NY: Time Books, 2016.

June E. O'Neill and Dave M. O'Neill. *The Declining Importance of Race and Gender in the Labor Market: The Role of Employment Discrimination Policies.* Washington, DC: AEI Press, 2012.

Paula S. Roghenberg, ed. *Race, Class, and Gender in the United States: An Integrated Study.* New York, NY: Worth, 2010.

Hanna Rosin. *The End of Men: And the Rise of Women.* New York, NY: Riverhead Books, 2012.

Sheryl Sandberg. *Lean In: Women, Work, and the Will to Lead.* New York, NY: Knopf, 2013.

Torild Skard. *Women of Power: Half a Century of Female Presidents and Prime Ministers Worldwide.* Bristol, UK: Policy Press, 2015.

Michele L. Swers. *Women in the Club: Gender and Policy Making in the Senate.* Chicago, IL: University of Chicago Press, 2013.

Sue Thomas and Clyde Wilcox, eds. *Women and Elective Office: Past, Present, and Future.* New York, NY: Oxford University Press, 2014.

## Periodicals and Internet Sources

Molly Ball, "A Woman's Edge," *Atlantic*, May 2013, Vol. 311, Issue 4, p. 15.

Keith Cunningham-Parmeter, "(Un)Equal Protection: Why Gender Equality Depends on Discrimination," *Northwestern University Law Review*, Fall 2014.

Blaze R. Douglas, "The Name of the Game Is Politics, and the Rules Are Forever Changed," *Woman Advocate,* Fall 2015, Vol. 21, Issue 1, p. 2.

Danny Hayes, Jennifer Lawless, and Gail Baitinger,"Who Cares What They Wear? Media, Gender, and the Influence of Candidate Appearance," *Social Science Quarterly*, December 2014, Vol. 95, Issue 5, pp. 1194–1212.

M. Margaret McKeown, "Beginning with Brown: Springboard for Gender Equality and Social Change," *San Diego Law Review,* September 1, 2015.

Kimberly Saks McManaway, "Domestication Without Representation: The Good Mother and the Gender Gap in Political Participation," *Conference Papers—Southern Political Science Association*, 2016, pp. 1–17.

Cynthia Terrell, "We Need to Do More Than Fix the Pipeline to Get Parity for Women in Office," *The Nation*, June 19, 2015.

Danielle Thomsen, "Why So Few (Republican) Women? Explaining the Partisan Imbalance of Women in the U.S. Congress," *Legislative Studies Quarterly*, May 2015, Vol. 40, Issue 2, pp. 295–323.

Katie Fischer Ziegler, "The Glass Dome," *State Legislatures,* July/August 2015, Vol. 41, Issue 7, pp. 20–25.

# Index